Anthony Amaral studied dressage under James Fillis, Jr., one of the finest horsemen of Europe and son of a former director of the Russian Cavalry School. He has since trained horses at the Kellogg Arabian Horse Ranch in California, managed an Arabian Horse ranch in Arizona, and still finds time to do some horse training and instruction. The author of four books and several hundred magazine articles (all about horses), Mr. Amaral lives with his wife in Santa Barbara, California.

HOW TO
TRAIN
YOUR
HORSE

ANTHONY AMARAL

HOW TO TRAIN YOUR HORSE

A COMPLETE GUIDE TO MAKING AN HONEST HORSE

WINCHESTER PRESS

Library of Congress Cataloging in Publication Data

Amaral, Anthony A   1930–
    How to train your horse.
    Includes index.
    1. Horse-training.   I. Title.
SF287.A42   636.1'08'86   77-1465
ISBN 0-87691-193-9

3 4 5 6 7   84 83 82 81 80

Printed in the United States of America

Published by Winchester Press
1421 S. Sheridan
Tulsa, Oklahoma 74112

THIS BOOK IS DEDICATED TO MY PARENTS, WHO
SHARE WITH ME SPECIAL HORSE MEMORIES OF
LONG AGO

ACKNOWLEDGMENTS

From my students I have learned much of the ever-different shades of rapport that develop between an individual and his horse, and that the training of a horse is a personal attainment in harmony. Particularly, I want to thank those students who helped in the making of this book.

ARLENE OTTO
DANA MITCHELL
ROBIN HERRMANN
ARLONDO THORNBURG

And special thanks to my wife, Jean, who read, edited and typed. Moreover, she held a guiding rein on me when I became vague or assumed more from the novice than was fair.

PHOTOGRAPHY BY JAMES D. TOMS

METHOD CANNOT GOVERN EVERYTHING; IT
LEADS EVERYBODY UP TO A CERTAIN POINT.

JOURNAL OF EUGÈNE DELACROIX

CONTENTS

INTRODUCTION

This book is designed to show you a way to train your horse. Granted, hundreds of books, booklets, magazine articles—even records—have offered similar advice ever since Xenophon wrote his thoughts on the subject in the fourth century B.C.

Many of these instructions, however, are written by professional horsemen for other professional horsemen. Details are often only implied, and, while understood by the professionals, leave the beginner with only fragmentary information.

For example: How many books discuss *feel*—a sense of intuitiveness—which is the dividing line between an accomplished horseman and an ordinary one? I can assure you that very few instruction manuals have bothered to discourse on the *feel* of horsemanship. In later chapters, means for developing this essential trait will be discussed.

While the classic works on horsemanship are marvelous excursions through centuries of ideas and techniques for training horses—from Xenophon to Pluvinel, Newcastle, Caprilli, Fillis, Chamberlain, Podhajsky—and offer much, they nevertheless represent whole systems of training. *This wholeness includes the particular temperament and abilities of those particular horsemen, and not necessarily your particular temperament or ability.* Essentially, the appeal and highest value in the classic works are to the experienced horseman.

The novice—the absolute newcomer to the realm of horses—is lost if he or she attempts to copy the methods of the great equestrian names. More likely the individual is on a road to discouragement (not to mention possible agony for the horse) rather than success.

Why?

Most books on training can show you only *a way* to train, but not necessarily *your way*, which evolves from *your own experiences, your own temperament, your own abilities*.

Secondly, only through the horse can you gain experience and develop your own awareness and skill in handling horses. Only by riding, training and handling as many different horses as possible will you find your own special abilities and skills. But all this is contingent on never underestimating the horse and its nature.

I recall a person telling me that training horses shouldn't be too difficult since the horse is a stupid animal. This superficial judgment depends on how one defines stupidity, and under what conditions it is measured. Scientific laboratory procedures have not rated the horse high on the animal intelligence scale. However, this measurement is purely academic. If a person is around horses long enough, and particularly if working from their backs, he comes to realize that the horse is one of the shrewdest, keenest animals alive in its relationship to man. Additionally, those people who think of horses as stupid animals are the same people who end up being easily fooled, baffled and defeated by the horse.

All this points to one of the few absolute rules about training horses. Remember it anytime you start to lose your temper or blame the horse for lack of intelligence when you fail to communicate. YOUR HORSE IS YOUR BEST CRITIC. The quality of his training is a direct result of your technique, your patience and your consideration of the horse's nature. Do not rationalize. Your horse mirrors you. And while, for the most part, horses are willing to accommodate your demands, if sensibly issued, they will fight when befuddled, abused or made wary.

Rephrasing the first sentence of this introduction, the purpose of this book is to help you develop your training abilities. The book will not offer an entire course in training the English or Western Pleasure horse; rather, it will present a system of basic training which allows you to develop your training technique and an understanding of the horse's thinking. If you apply yourself (and I will be repetitious in explaining those fundamental ideas that improve abilities) you will establish solid training procedures. From here you may carry on for yourself and explore other books on horsemanship with better comprehension.

My approach is based on years of training and working with young people (and older ones too) who wished to
be more involved with their horses by training them. I'll
not only explain *how*, but *how to correct* when the horse
doesn't comply. For example, take lunging. We all know
how a horse is supposed to lunge, ideally; but what if the
horse will not go out to the end of the line? Or stops? Or
faces the handler? Or comes in? Or runs wildly at the end
of the line, having its own way and establishing a bad
habit (not to mention the possible temper tantrum from its
handler)? In those moments, when the horse turns tricky
and evasive, your training ability is truly challenged.

Not only must you know what to do, but you must
react in accordance with the peculiarities of the horse's
nature. Thus, there will be considerable discussion on this
matter before actual training procedures are dealt with.
Don't skip these preliminaries. After all, working a horse is
not like hopping on a bike and riding off. The horse is a
living, emotional being, and the more you understand its
habits and peculiarities, the better you will control it
through training.

Years ago, when I was studying dressage under James
Fillis, Jr., a son of the former director of the Russian
Cavalry School and one of the finest horsemen of Europe,
he said to me: "If you will think, I will show you a way to
train. If you will continue to think, you will find your own
way further than I can show you, and you will be your own
horseman."

I offer you the same invitation.

ANTHONY AMARAL
Santa Barbara, California
January, 1977

CHAPTER

1

A PHILOSOPHIC APPROACH

Before you cringe at the word philosophic, let me assure you it is used here only to serve certain ideas about training that are attitudes rather than specific procedures.

Actually, the purpose of this chapter is to present a broad spectrum of training ideas and some of the initial pitfalls that frequently confront the novice. Following this overview, we'll concentrate on a few items requiring clarification.

You may believe, after the introduction, that I have disparaged horse training books. I haven't, actually. Matter of fact, my own library on horse books would cause one to assume I am a bibliomaniac on horse books. What I want to emphasize, however, is that one must maintain a particular perspective about them. After all, it isn't fair to authors if you assume that all one has to do is follow what they write and presto—a trained horse.

I know many amateurs have followed this path and finally thrown up their hands in confusion while uttering some harsh invective at the author. But this is because they expected more than the book could possibly provide. Generally, knowing what a book cannot do for you will give you an awareness of what you have to learn on your own.

In any case, compliment yourself if you have followed the teachings of books. It indicates much about your attitude—certainly the desire to learn, and to act rightly for your horse by sparing it discomfort and pain. This approach, at least, has a nobility that is lacking in individuals who get on a horse and, by "booting" and "yanking," force the horse into responses.

Nonetheless, even if Sherlock Holmes had become interested in horse training, I'm sure even he would have been muddled by the conflicting book advice.

He would not have stood alone—neither in his time nor the present. More than ever there is, along with the phenomenal growth of the number of horses and interest in horses, the desire by novices to train their own. It's a wonderful motivation and, I assure you, more enhancing to one's love and appreciation of horses.

This motivation to train appears stronger in the West than the East; yet, the frustrations are the same for many who rely strictly on book instruction. For unless an individual develops rapport—an emotional affinity between himself and the horse—no set of instructions will suffice even on the most basic level.

Rapport is a key attainment to strive for, and reflects the sense of *feel* previously mentioned. *Feel* is difficult to explain. It's almost beyond intellectualization. It does begin with remembering, always, and especially in moments of training troubles, not to expect the horse to think as you do. You must learn to slant your thinking to the horse's, which is a mode of reacting rather than reasoning. In fact, the horse's reasoning powers are limited. What's more, the horse, regardless of his size, is essentially a timid animal (fortunately!). For eons of time, ever since the horse was no larger than a collie dog, nature has set its mind to run—not to reason—whenever danger was evident. The solid hoof, the set of the eye, which allowed the horse to see almost all about him even while grazing, and his keen sense of smell and hearing, are all nature's survival mechanisms to afford the horse the best advantages to get away from danger.

This instinct to run when frightened is strong among horses to one degree or another. Here's an example, and one that often causes people to consider the horse stupid. It happens every day at a hitching post or rail: A horse pulls back on the halter. We might believe the sensible reaction from the horse would be to stop pulling, since the halter is bound to be pinching behind its ears and causing it pain. But what the horse usually does is pull back even harder, practically in a panic, until the halter or the shank breaks.

Stupid?

Only by our reasoning. For the horse, in that moment when he felt the pressure pain, he became frightened, and set back even harder to escape the pain. He wasn't reasoning; instinct was telling him to get away!

Yet, I have seen, as probably you have, horse handlers

lose their temper at this display of horse "stupidity" and even punish the horse. One might as well call a rock stupid and yell at it.

Better than losing one's temper and frightening the horse even more with a harsh, "Here! Quit that!" would be to play a game of *as if*. This is a technique sometimes used by doctors working with mental patients. When a patient acts up, the doctor reacts as if it did not happen and avoids making a bigger issue of the matter. This works many times with horses. I've had them pull back on the halter while being groomed, and instead of making an issue of it, I merely stood quietly, and they stopped pulling. Maybe this seems contradictory to my previous statement about horses pulling back even harder, but it only points out, as you will learn, that exceptions abound in horse behavior. Sometimes a method will work, sometimes it will not. But as I will discuss later, one's actions around horses, even the most casual, are a form of training and conditioning. Playing the *as if* game, I've learned, has had a calming effect on horses in their moments of panic.

Now, let us return to your learning how to comprehend the horse's behavior and thinking. This understanding is important whether teaching a colt to lead at halter or undertaking the most advanced training. Many of the horse's habits and thought patterns are quickly grasped if you stay alert; watch its mannerisms and think about its reactions to you. An understanding of the horse's particular thinking becomes the very skeleton on which training principles build.

Training, by nature, is simple: A horse is capable of learning because of innate reflexes. A horse could not be taught, for example, to canter, jump, perform a lofty passage, or even curl its upper lip in a smile if it did not already have that ability. But it is the technique and the talent—the rapport—of the trainer which determines the ease with which he elicits these responses, and, in turn, the degree of perfection in the horse's performance.

A horse is conditioned to desired responses by reward—either the cessation of an aid (or the firmness with which it is applied), or some mechanical action upon the horse. Often this diminishing of an aid is accompanied by making much over the horse as a form of reward. The ceasing of the aid, or its pressure, reinforces the horse's mental attitude to respond in the way that brought the immediate ceasing of the aid. And so there is established at that moment a desired training response from the horse.

The more repetitious the aid and the response by the horse, the more readily the horse acts out the response as a habit of behavior. Keep this always in mind: The horse is a habit-loving animal. It feels secure, comfortable, in routine procedures. But—*a horse will learn bad habits even more readily if a trainer fails to use patience* (causing a horse to defend itself) *or is awkward or uncertain in the presentation of his method.* All of which is again another way of saying— *lacking in rapport.*

Therefore, the horse's habit-like nature is a trainer's best leverage. On the other hand, it is also the horse's best defense against improper handling, which may force him into an attempt to buck, rear, run away, strike or bite.

Simple?

Yes and no.

Yes, because the principles are quickly understood. *No,* because the application of these principles is derived from a lifetime spent learning the subtleties of training horses; of gauging the temperament, disposition and intelligence of individual horses and matching a training technique accordingly. This is both the frustration and fascination in the study of horse training, and proves the impossibility of books serving completely as a successful method for the novice.

Consequently, only by gaining experience that develops into a personal style can the trainer then recognize other ideas that have significance and meaning. Thus, there are a number of ways to train a horse to a similar end, and attempting to copy another's method without consideration of one's own limitations may bring forth more pitfalls than advantages.

All right. Enough theory for the moment. Let's look at

some actual examples which illuminate, perhaps, the sort of dilemma you may have faced.

A case in point is the book, *Breaking and Riding*, by James Fillis, Sr. Now Fillis was world-renowned in dressage and high school riding, although some of his techniques are not taken seriously today. At one time his reputation and his book exerted enormous influence on the trainers of horses. Only a few, however, were able to duplicate his methods. And those few were outstanding horsemen who used Fillis as a guide to compare, perhaps adjust, their own theories on training.

Novices have attempted to copy Fillis, since he was an equestrian hero of the sort others wished to be. Fillis's techniques of teaching collection from the ground (as opposed to teaching from the saddle) resulted in horses that were behind the bit (a dangerous evasiveness in the horse) rather than collected and on the bit. In many cases, the horses were ruined. No idle chitchat was intended when one critic said that the Fillis method (particularly for beginners) was literally a razor in the hands of a monkey.

Let us examine two more instances—one with an Eastern flavor and the other with a Western.

In the East, and certainly throughout much of Europe, comparisons are often made between the Italian and German schools of training and equitation. It's a debate which flares periodically, and perhaps while not as intense as this writer remembers it, still serves for comparative purposes to show the contradictions which confuse novices.

The Italian mode of equitation has traditionally— since the time of its innovator, Caprilli—relied on a more natural way of riding; that is, a free-moving horse developing its own balance under the forward seat style of riding for cross-country and jumping. The snaffle is the primary bit. Collection is minimal and dressage employed is on an elementary level.

The German system, on the other hand, relies considerably on dressage. Much collection is demanded through a double bridle, and absolute control is vested in the rider.

Each system represents divergent techniques—one generally allowing a free-going style with the horse, and the other far more regulatory. Yet both systems have produced winners in international competitions. Even more intriguing, each method is a deep reflection of the temperament of the nationalities. This *temperament* is one of the important variables. It is not to be lightly passed over when studying techniques for one's own use.

Even in the American West the historic manners of American horsemen display divergent techniques. The *Californio* system of training stock horses with hackamore and spade bit is miles apart, literally and figuratively, from the Texas way, with snaffles and grazer bits. The old time *Californios* with their centerfire saddles and quick-reining stock horses followed a cultural heritage handed down for generations, and an environmental philosophy which responded to *no se apure*—don't be in a hurry.

Horses were worked in a hackamore for about two years while learning the maneuvers of the stock horse. More time was spent in the four-reins—hackamore and spade bit. Eventually the horse graduated to the spade bit. Perhaps four years were required for the horse to reach the high standards of the *Californio's* art of the reining horse, with lightning quick responses to the slightest manipulation of the reins and weight of the rider.

The horses of the California vaqueros have considerable similarity to German-trained horses in the control and precision practiced by both.

In Texas, different ideas were molded to the making of a cow horse. With an attitude that was typically Anglo-American, stock horse training was strictly utilitarian. Texans took all the short cuts in getting a horse reasonably capable for working cattle. *No se apure* had little meaning in that part of America. Working cattle was strictly business, and the horse a tool. So the cutting horse evolved, and his training resembled the Italian system in the idea of leniency and few controls.

While these comparisons are overly simplified, they

do illustrate the different ways horses can be trained to similar purposes. A novice comparing the Texan and the Far West styles of stock horse training usually asks—which is the better method?

Actually it makes no difference. The more important question is—which method should a novice choose to follow if he wishes to train a stock horse?

Assuming that each system was unadulterated, one would be forced to work the Texas system simply because the vaquero's art is too difficult to comprehend without considerable experience. Moreover, the subtle *feel* is imperative in working a spade bit. Yet, how many unfortunate horses are put in spade bits simply because an ignorant rider used it strictly for its leverage to control a hardmouthed horse?

Today, shades of all systems of training are evident in show ring performances. Moreover, it is this multiple shading of training styles which causes confusion in novice trainers searching for perspective.

And this is just the beginning of the confusion. He or she may read that lunging is the best way to work a young horse. Another writer advocates driving. Still another says, *Get on and ride, since that is what you have to do sooner or later.* This lets loose many conflicting theories as one moves along in examining training methods.

And so, the newcomer, and the not-so-newcomer, is beset by an avalanche of ideas and contradictions on techniques and equipment. There is no simple solution to ease the way, except that one must begin to think. For the simple matter of it all is that there are good ideas in all approaches—humane ones, that is. But the effectiveness of a method depends on one's abilities.

The method we will eventually discuss will allow the novice to develop his ability, and build his confidence. That way, the horse stands a better chance of being trained.

A HORSE IS A HORSE — AND NOT A DOG

An attitude, the dictionary tells us, is a mental position or feeling with regard to an object.

It is your attitude, your posture and habits around horses, that I want to discuss, since I feel certain that our actions with horses, in the casual, everyday relationship, is a form of training and conditioning.

You might feel offended at what I have to say about human behavior with horses, and believe that I am being excessive in my opinions. Maybe I am. Still, I want to offer this point of view so it will be part of your further awareness about horses.

Let me start with a comparison to dogs. I'm convinced that many dog lovers have made neurotics of their pets. Overpampering, overfeeding, and worse, overhumanizing, have made many fat, lazy and dull dogs. Probably ranch and bird dogs, sheep dogs and a few others are the last of their species performing in a capacity that gives them a reason for enjoying life.

Fortunately, horses haven't been as overindulged as the dog. And while the house-pet dog can live with the inactive role we have imposed upon it because it is more affectionate to man, the horse has little of that same affection or attachment displayed by the canine.

Yet, as the horse emerges more and more as a hobby or pleasure animal rather than a working partner of man, which characterized its role in the age of horse culture (before the combustion engine), I have seen a tendency in many horse lovers to expect and encourage their horses to respond as pets. It's silly, and it can be dangerous.

Now don't misread me. Horses are a joy to be with. To have fun with them is part of the reason for keeping them. But to force or even expect a pet-like responsiveness from them is a disfavor to the animal. It can make them disagreeable and, I repeat, even dangerous.

Writing this, I know, is almost a heresy. And while I am aware that many horses respond to—or maybe a better word is *endure*—too much fondling and hugging, there are many more who back my argument against overpampering. Certainly the horse appreciates kind treatment, and most enjoy having humans about. But the horse has limits.

Here's an example: A young girl—really, she was the epitome of the crazy-over-horses syndrome—had a good-looking, alert, half-Thoroughbred mare. The girl spent endless hours with the mare, riding and grooming her and petting her endlessly on the face, ears and muzzle. No horse, I'm sure, ever had more attention. But little by little, the horse displayed annoyance over this pampering and fondling. It would lay its ears back, jerking its head away when the girl attempted to pet. Then came the nipping. That should have been sufficient warning. The girl, however, merely admonished the horse with a gentle voice. To the horse, that soft tone was an encouragement, and before long it began to take lunges at her. Instead of the girl easing off her coddling habits, she made a game of tag out of the mare's lunging. Every time the horse lunged, the girl jumped back, and before long she had the mare chasing her, and it looked like a trained trick. The girl was delighted. (The habit could have been developed into a trick, except the girl didn't understand how to make the horse aware of its limits when performing it.)

One day when the mare was trotting behind the girl, she encouraged the game by reaching back at the horse's face and then sprinting away. This time the game ended with the girl being hospitalized, for the mare, at the end of its patience, snaked out its head and clamped its teeth into the flesh above her hipbone.

When I was told of this, I impressed the girl's mother that not only did the horse need discipline, but the daughter must change her habit of petting and playing games with the mare. Unfortunately, stern punishment was required before the horse became relatively docile again and receptive to good training methods. She was certainly not given any more opportunities at trying her strength against humans.

Remember, a horse is intelligent enough to be trained, but, fortunately, does not have the wits to realize its own powers or use them against man, *unless it is encouraged.*

Another way of improperly handling your horse with overindulgence and mistaken kindness is by overfeeding it with rich feeds not warranted for the amount of work the horse is doing. Feeding your horses must be in accordance to the individual animal's needs. Granted, some require more feed than others, and can handle great amounts of rich feed without their personality being affected. Others can be overfed with just small amounts of rich feed. They turn skittish and develop bad habits such as chewing stall doors or fences. Rich feeds require that the horse be given ample work to offset the rich diet. Otherwise, some horses—excuse the expression—begin to feel their oats and can become bold enough to intimidate their owners.

Many times, I feel these attitudes of novices around horses stem from uncertainty about how to establish the appropriate relationship (again—rapport!) with a horse. In that uncertainty, there is the tendency to grant the horse the benefit of the doubt and overindulge him. Remember: THE HORSE QUICKLY SENSES THE DEGREE OF CONFIDENCE IN AN INDIVIDUAL. They learn quickly to size up a person and will take advantage of any weaknesses they discover. The horse likes nothing better than having its own way. The more it is allowed, the more it enforces that behavioral pattern.

Here is another example: A family I know started to raise foals from a mare that was their first venture into horses and horse breeding. When I became acquainted with them they had a three-year-old stallion out of the mare. The mare had lost her next foal, and when I arrived in order to work the stallion the following year, she was again in foal.

The point is this: The young stallion was the only other horse on the premises and had received exceptional treatment and led a self-ordained life. In three years all he had learned was to wear a halter and be led about. He knew no other discipline and was allowed to go his own way. When the family first began trying to groom him, he began to paw the ground and would not stand still. The family, ignorant about such matters, slacked off the grooming. The horse had won. When they tried to pick up his legs to clean his hoofs, he would jerk with his leg and get loose, or lean heavily on the person. He won again. This slight misbehavior was dismissed by the family in the belief the horse was too young to mind and he would settle down as he got older.

Remember, all this started from coltish days. Instead of the family insisting that the horse learn manners and behave (even though it was a colt), it was permitted to get away with its recalcitrant behavior.

I'm not criticizing this family. They are one of thousands of amateurs who need advice—especially about stallions—and some help. So, the horse had had little discipline and no conditioning as to what his role was supposed to be.

He was also a pet. He was played with by the kids, encouraged to come running across the pasture to a waiting tidbit, and started nipping when there were no more tidbits. At night he would stand in his stall and bang his knees against the door until he was let out.

As I have indicated, when I met the family and their young stallion, he was a menace. He had never had a hand laid on him for discipline and had no tolerance for anything that did not satisfy the way he was conditioned to behave. Farriers, I learned, had a devil of a time with him. One threw the stallion and tied its legs in order to trim its hoofs. The family thought that was cruel and never recalled that particular farrier, although being thrown was probably the best lesson that horse had in respecting humans.

In essence, however, this horse had no respect, or fear, of people. Try to put a halter on him and he would twist his neck back to take a nip. Once, when I started handling him and was putting on his halter (after I had already elbowed him a few times when he attempted to nip at me) he suddenly dropped to his knees and attempted to bite my lower leg.

When I first mounted him he offered no resistance. But no urgings would make him move forward. I squeezed with my calves, then used my heels, then kicked. All he did was grunt and become restive. I felt that soon he would start to rear and that put fear into me. So, I allowed a member of the family to lead him while I was mounted. He moved easily, simply because being led was one response that he had learned and accepted as natural. But when I again attempted to make him move by using my legs, he balked. It was imperative that I make him move forward, so I decided to use a riding crop. As I used my legs I popped him on the rump as well. He almost flew from under the saddle. And for about twenty seconds he rampaged around the pasture. But—he had moved!

A week later, with consistent use of stern punishment whenever he refused to obey my heels, he began acting like a horse that has learned to defer to human wishes.

Today, this horse is a gelding and one of the gentlest I know. Yet, when I was working him, I considered him one of the most dangerous animals I have ever handled; dangerous because he had learned virtually no discipline. Worse, and I repeat, he had no respect—call it fear, if you wish—for people. Unfortunately, he had to go through a rough time with me, but there was no choice. And all because of overpampering and lack of basic discipline.

When I see other horses on the verge of this sort of behavior, usually caused by owners spoiling them, I cringe. It is annoying to me to see people who insist upon kissing their horses, bringing foals into the house, and, worst of all, allowing horses to get away with minor indiscretions because they do not have the heart to punish or discipline. These people insist they will not be cruel to their animals. But they're doing the horse no favor. Future punishment of the horse will probably be many times more severe. It will have to be, in order to break dangerous habits unwittingly brought on by overindulgent owners.

Pardon the cliché, but an ounce of prevention *is* worth a pound of cure—especially in the training of horses. So be careful of treating your horse like you would treat your dog. The horse does not respond like a dog. Nature did not develop him that way. A horse's slight nips, slight misbehavior when having his hoofs cleaned or trimmed, or a slight bucking, can quickly progress to powerful tactics once the horse learns how effectively they will work for him. Remember, to the horse, there is no distinction between what is a good habit or a bad habit. All are the same to him.

Now you don't have to be armed with a stout whip each time you approach your horse to prove your dominance over him. If you will develop a calm attitude, be firm and confident with him, he will respond in deference to your judgment and demands. This is, as I said in the beginning, a form of conditioning, or training, based on your habits and postures around the horse.

Since I will be talking in depth on the matter of punishment in the next chapter, I will only briefly describe here the meaning of firmness to illustrate the idea behind all horse handling. I will use the foal for an example. This is the stage when horses are most reluctant to being conditioned to forms of discipline, and also when good and bad habits are encouraged.

Usually, after a foal is a few months old, or after weaning, basic handling begins. Picking up each leg to clean the hoof often causes a foal to struggle and jerk its legs, especially the hind. It's a natural response. With gentling words, you should continue to try to pick up the leg and hold it for a few moments even though the foal will probably struggle harder, and probably get loose again. But without resorting to harsh commands or slaps on the rump (which only make the foal more frightened, defensive and stronger), keep picking up the leg, speaking softly, until the foal ceases its struggle—if only for a moment. Then gently let its leg down. You have now established an impression—that when it ceased struggling, even for that one moment, it was released— unharmed.

Repetition is the keynote. Follow this procedure over and over—always remaining *calm, confident* and *firm*— and quickly the colt will allow his leg to be lifted without undue concern, and will do the same when he is grown and stronger. He has been taught to submit to this particular demand as a *matter of habit* because he loves habit and is habit-oriented.

And so it is, also, if you allow unfavorable habits to develop because of excessive pampering and spoiling. The process of habit-forming depends on what you let develop. Be watchful for those signs in your behavior around horses that encourage undesirable responses, and discipline accordingly. Remember, while you love horses, also to respect them. Never permit the horse to use its size and strength against you.

CHAPTER
3

THE HONEST HORSE

In the so-called golden age of horse training when, as in all golden ages, a particular perfection evolved before the bottom fell out and nothing was ever the same again, horse trainers proudly guarded their training techniques. Some of the more enterprising, like Rarey, made international reputations by displaying the results—not the secret—of taming bad-tempered horses by mysterious methods.

Others, all experts in understanding the nature of horses, published their methods under such titillating titles as *The Secret of Taming Horses*. Or, *So and So's Method of Developing Gentle Horses—Revealed for the First Time!* One successful item was a booklet on how to break horses of bad habits. Its enormous yearly sales indicates that many horses were probably poorly managed and that perhaps the golden age of horse training was not so golden after all.

Today, one rarely hears of such *secrets* being offered for sale, or of trainers displaying silly vanity by suggesting they have special and mysterious knowledge for use in training horses. Yet there is one secret—if it can be called such. Successful trainers know and rely on it for turning out nicely trained and mannered horses. The secret? Select the proper horse for the distinctive training in which the horse will be involved.

No top trainer is going to take a high-headed, high-stepping and excitable Saddlebred and turn it into a cutting horse. And by the same token he will not use a short-legged, heavily-muscled Quarter Horse and develop a streamlined English Pleasure horse. These are exaggerations, of course, and actually they *can* be done in unusual instances. But the possibility of ease and success in training are much greater when the trainer selects that animal whose conformation, breeding or bloodlines display an aptitude suitable to English Pleasure or to cutting.

The novice, too, should be selective. But curiously enough, the one ingredient in a horse's make-up that is least considered by novices is the one most important.

That is the horse's disposition. Color, size and markings tend to be the main attractions to people in their beginning fascination with horses.

Let me relate a story. Remember the tale of how Alexander—before his name was plumed with *the Great*— tamed the excitable Bucephalus? The black, wild-eyed stallion reared and plunged against his merchant handlers, causing Alexander's father to dismiss the horse as an addition to the royal stable. Youthful Alexander interceded. Merely by turning Bucephalus' head into the sun and away from the darting shadows of his handlers, and his own, Alexander calmed the magnificent charger. There was nothing wrong with the horse, we are led to believe, other than those nasty shadows.

Actually, there was probably much amiss with a horse that reared at shadows, and although the story leans heavily on legend, the scene does have a certain reality. For when a person is young, as was Alexander, there is a fascination, indescribable, with the gentling of high-spirited horses.

I once felt it when mounting an excitable, cavorting horse. He challenged my tact and ability (which, then, was more bluff) and my sense of manliness. In some cases, my common sense was in arrest. Today I shy away from zany horses. More importantly, I now place disposition first in judging a horse for purchase or training. I'll even overlook some conformation faults in favor of a horse with a level-headed and kindly disposition.

Certainly I do not dislike all high-spirited horses. After all, it is this very quality that makes champions in horse show classes. And who can deny the absolute beauty of an animated, spirited horse at liberty? But the distinguishing point between the highly spirited horse that is relatively safe and the highly spirited that is unsafe is honesty of its disposition.

Honesty is a human designation and, naturally, meaningless to the horse, since he does not rationalize. But since a horse can injure, even kill, its rider, a term like honesty is appropriate for calculating a horse's temperament or disposition.

In the past decade I have kept records of people hurt by horses. I don't mean the usual accidents like falling off or being stepped on, but instances where horses were out of control. In about sixty percent of those cases, where I could examine the horse personally, I found the animal to be a type that was overly impetuous. These horses displayed temperaments which, when suddenly frightened, moved them to trust to nothing but their most primitive instinct. They would flee, and, not unlikely, charge into a fence or into highway traffic or anything else which was contrary to their own safety. Other horses, also lacking an amiable disposition, easily learned evasive habits such as rearing, running backwards or bucking when their riders asked for even simple responses. Unfortunately, horses of this type can be purchased cheaply—and, if I may say so, usually by horse-struck girls. Although they may be warned that they will be over-horsed, they feel that kindness and patience will settle the horse.

Maybe. But aside from the risks involved in purchasing a poorly disposed horse, there are too many more acceptable horses for sale (even if one must save a while longer). To waste time in the exhausting chore of retraining a spoiled horse, or attempting to change some basic mental structure in a horse that is not inclined toward enjoying humans, is foolish. Much better to seek one with an honest temperament.

What, then, is an *honest horse*?

Simply, an honest horse is the opposite in behavior mentioned above. The honest horse's life is not a continuous spooking at everything, real or imagined, or fighting efforts to ride him, even though he may have been forced into such behavior by poor or misguided treatment. More important, the honest horse defers his primitive instincts to his rider, and this is called *confidence*.

(On this term, *confidence*, let me digress a moment.

Gaining a horse's confidence and the other phrase about using patience when training are two expressions found in virtually any book on horse training. But *patience* and *confidence*—and the latter grows out of the former—might as well be written in Greek since, generally speaking, they are the two things least practiced by American horsemen—and particularly by novices. The American horseman has a characteristic impatience. He's a rusher, a searcher for short cuts, and while this may be harmless in certain pursuits, it will not be compromised by the horse. Maybe our hurrying of horses is forced by our anxiety to get the horse ready for the show, our impatience to see results. Whatever the reasons, they are self-defeating. You have only to witness enough horse shows to note the unruly, agitated, half-trained horses in the show ring.)

Certainly, the honest horse can also be high-strung, spook on occasion, and may even put up a scrap during his training, but if his disposition to misbehavior is within a sensible range, he is not basically restive. His instinct is to go forward and submit to his rider's will. He responds to an encouraging voice, or to a rider who transmits assuredness through a firm seat and educated hands that understand the bit and its relationship to the horse's mouth in communicating steadiness.

If these qualities are lacking in a rider, especially on a high-spirited horse, the rider's hesitance—his lack of confidence—will be sensed by the horse, who will also lose confidence. And he will in turn react in his own best interests. But the rider, even the novice, at least has a chance with an honest horse. The opposite type, having a basic disposition fault, gives little of himself, or any hope for his rider to enjoy the experience or build his own confidence.

Disposition is the overall temperament and personality of the horse. His ability to be trained and his capacity to be enjoyed depends greatly on whether or not he has an honest disposition.

I remember Fat Jones, when he was the largest supplier of horses for motion pictures, stating that he might look at a hundred horses before he found one suitable for the business of working in front of the cameras. He was speaking of star horses that frequently work at liberty. Beauty was important. So was spirit. But unless the horse had the disposition to take cues reliably from his trainer, and keep cool in the hectic surroundings of movie-making, neither beauty nor spirit would sustain him in a film career.

In addition, a good-natured horse will accept some mistakes in his training, even some abuse, without altering his disposition or temperament. He will come back with a basic cheerfulness and willingness. However, a bad-natured horse sours. His suspiciousness is strengthened, along with his tendency to self-reliance, which often means fighting for his own way. And where a highly spirited horse with a good disposition can be lunged if he is too edgy, rarely does an equal amount of lunge work change the attitude of the other type. He virtually has to be lunged into exhaustion.

Another reason why the dishonest horse should be avoided is because little can be done to change his particular mental patterns. There is no fine dividing line between good- and bad-tempered horses. It is a matter of degree, which assumes more varied shadings according to the particular abilities of the rider or trainer handling the horse. Some horses never change and are nuisances as long as they live. Others may sour and remain so under one handler, but improve their personalities with more sympathetic handling. Some horses seemingly never become nasty even though they may have reason to. Other types, when young, display repulsive attitudes, but calm into pleasing dispositions as they age.

Horses may not be intelligent as scientists gauge intelligence in animals, but their degrees of temperament are extensive and not to be dismissed easily if one's experience with horses is minimal. Fortunately, just as a horse has no idea he can be repugnant (by human measurement), neither does he try to hide his particular behaviorisms.

The eye of the horse tells much about disposition. (This assumption, by the way, as with so many other aspects of the horse's nature and his training, has exceptions.) If a horse has large, warm-looking eyes, he is probably a warm, honest, friendly type of an animal. But an eye that tends to glare, flits a lot, and shows much white (the white sclerotic rim), could reflect the other end of the disposition spectrum. *But not always.* Many horses will show white and display an excitable nature, yet still be *honest* horses and perhaps develop into animated and classy performers. But other horses, because of this sclerotic rim development, may see more than their minds can accommodate or understand, and react with mannerisms that are fidgety, nervous and distrustful. More certainly, be wary of a horse with pig-like eyes, Roman nose (an exaggerated convex line to the face) or ears that constantly flit back and forth (indicating nervousness) or lay back (indicating hostility).

Overall, the best way to test a horse's disposition is to study him a while. Even a novice can detect some indications of a horse's temperament and personality by either working the horse out or having someone else ride the horse for them to observe. And insist, whether you are riding or watching, that the horse be steamed up in a workout in order to see its behavior while under pressure.

There is neither common sense nor pleasure in being overhorsed, or in having a horse that is literally smarter than its rider or handler. But enjoyment begins with a horse whose disposition is manageable within one's own abilities. Needless to emphasize, it is the only sort of horse for a novice to begin learning how to train.

PUNISHMENT AND TRAINING PERSUASION

A horseman of the old California vaquero school of horse training once summed up for me his special approach to handling horses: "*Ni azucar ni espuela cada dis.*"

Neither sugar nor spur every day. It means much more than just the sum of the words. Inherent in that expression is one of those pragmatic procedural codes of the astute horseman: *Avoid extremes!*

Previously, we looked at possible results of the "sugar-syndrome" extreme, the over-pampering of the horse which might create undesirable habits. Casually implied was the idea of punishment. But its proper use in training the horse is another mark of the astute horseman. For unless you can communicate your ideas to the horse, and in a manner made easy for him to understand, then you are not training.

Punishment is an inexact word to apply to training because of its negative connotations. Discipline also short-changes the idea, since it implies correction after the fact. Persuasion is a better word, but it also requires the meanings of punishment and discipline to fulfill the intention of training. So, in this chapter I want to form the basic theory behind the skill in persuading horses to make trained responses.

Obviously, one cannot talk to horses in the literal sense. Tone of voice, however, is definitely a form of communication. Mellow utterances communicate assurance to the horse, and a satisfaction with a response you have received from him. Harsh utterances, on the other hand, are quickly recognized by the horse as a form of disapproval. The words are immaterial. You can use the foulest language known, but if it is said with soft tones the horse will have a sense of comfort and well-being. And the sweetest endearments in the language, if spoken stridently, will put the horse on guard.

Your voice—its tone—is an important adjunct to training. Learn to use it effectively—and this means consistently—as a training aid. Your horse will rapidly identify your tone with approval or disapproval of his manners or actions.

But voice is a secondary aid. To train a horse to a particular response requires a stronger aid, something the horse will respond to because that aid has caused some discomfort to his physical being. Very often this aid is a riding crop, and your ability to use it properly—with skill—is a good test of your proficiency as a trainer. Eventually, I'll talk about proper manipulating of whips, but let's see how the punishment-persuasion technique works.

Punishment, or persuasion, is how we communicate with the horse. Proper responses receive no punishment, and the horse is persuaded that what he did was correct. Improper responses receive a sting of reprimand and the horse learns not to give that particular response.

Unfortunately, the term punishment has almost as many meanings as readers of this page. So let's make our meaning as clear as possible. Xenophon, the ancient Greek, wrote, in what is considered the first surviving treatise on the horse: "Never approach a horse in passion, for anger never thinks of the consequences, and forces us to do what we afterwards regret. . . ." Read this over a few times. Think about it. It is one of those few absolute rules of training.

Punishment is disciplining, correcting, or teaching a lesson. It does not mean whipping or flogging from a loss of temper. This is cruelty, and especially so if the horse has no idea why he is being severely reprimanded. Also, anyone who adopts this practice isn't even as smart as the horse. That person has chosen to fight the horse on its own terms—flight and strength—and the horse is a lot faster and a lot stronger. The horse will rebel (remember what was said about its nature), and you can't train a rebellious horse. You can break its spirit, but you probably wouldn't have much left to work with. The horse will have lost interest, and his feeling of confidence in the trainer. The trainer loses all around.

Fortunately, outright cruelty is rare. Punishment, however, is part of the training process. When we speak of training, it includes punishment and reward. Yet, select almost any book written by an American and the phrase *reward and punishment* is mentioned too casually and too cursorily. American writers are a squeamish lot when compared to European writers, who are not word-mincers when they write on training of horses. James Fillis, that eminent French horseman of the last century, wrote: "Above all, the rider of a difficult horse should not lose his temper. When a horse deserves punishment, he should get it with an amount of severity which might be regarded as an outcome of anger. But I do not hesitate to say that it is better not to punish the horse than to punish too late."

There is much wisdom in Fillis's advice—worth rereading a few times. And notice key points: *severity,* meaning that the horse must know precisely that he has responded incorrectly—one sharp crack of the whip. Also, *punish immediately after the act.* A three-second delay on your part and the horse will not associate the punishment with the incorrect response, thus causing resentment toward you.

There are some who have said that Fillis was often rough with his horses. So was his son, whom I worked with. But they had to be. They demanded more from their horses in precise dressage and high school routines. Fillis advocated definite, strong punishment because no horse worth his salt block is going to submit to training demands docilely. And the more that is demanded—especially in pursuit of perfection—the more the horse will put up defenses. Horses can't be blamed for resisting; they see no reason for the many things that are dictated to them. When the horse does submit, he performs because he is obedient to learned cues. Obedience derives from discipline, and discipline from appropriate punishment; and the severity of the punishment depends on the horse and what you are attempting to teach him.

There are reservations concerning punishment. It can be overdone if one forgets that the techniques of *proper timing, repetition* and *consistency* in training also count in obtaining the desired response from the horse. These, together with *punishment* and *reward,* are the five important principles for training horses. Even the simplest training procedure is useless if these principles are not remembered and understood. (These five principles will be quickly learned by you in the procedures in ground training to be discussed later.)

If punishment is important, so is the ability to know when to use it and in what intensity for particular types of horses. The amount or degree of punishment used against a sullen, stubborn type would hardly be appropriate for the timid or excitable horse. Everything seems to frighten this latter type. His native instincts are close to the surface and he's ready to run and bolt. Punishment, obviously, would hardly serve as a strong measure in training this type. Patience, almost limitless, is needed with this particular temperament.

On the other hand, the stubborn horse respects a few hard knocks. This horse is usually thinking of ways to avoid duties and training and makes a constant habit of testing his rider or handler. Give him an inch and he will press his advantage for more.

These types represent extremes. They are not average horses in personality and disposition, and were mentioned to show the limits where punishment is mostly futile for one type and effective for the other.

The average horse—especially the one with a pleasant disposition—is intelligent, and, for the most part, willing. But don't be fooled. He can be evasive, too, and develop keen perceptions on how to make his work easier. Have you ever seen a horse who leaves the home area at a walk that suggests he might be pulling a borax wagon all by his lonesome·self? Then, when turned around and heading home, he walks faster than some horses trot? This is what I mean about recognizing the horse's ability—or potential—and knowing when he is testing you by half efforts. One or two sharp cracks with a riding crop would soon convince him that you expect a reasonably energetic walk when leaving the stable area.

There are other considerations regarding punishment. The horse is a creature of habit and feels a certain comfort and security in routine. It follows, then, that repetition in training procedures is important in order to impress any particular training upon the horse.

Still, as important as repetition is, it can also be the seed for some annoying habits on the part of the horse. Stock horses, for example, are quick to learn—because of routine repetition—that a run-and-slide, and a few off-sets, usually means the end of the routine and time to head back to the stall. This anticipation stimulates the horse to rush and become sloppy in his performance. And often he finds himself being punished. So, my point is this: *it is also important to know how to avoid situations that may require punishment of the horse.*

In order to prevent his anticipating the next move, vary the routine once it has been learned. After all, his anticipation frequently means he is trying to please you. It is unfair to punish him for a shortcoming in a well-versed routine unless you are certain he is just being stubborn. His failing could be caused by pain or discomfort, such as an improperly fitting bridle or a rubbing cinch. So, in a critical moment, you must determine the reason for the disobedience and decide what to do. Is there good reason for his mis-action, or is he just being stubborn?

First of all, let me repeat—CHECK THE EQUIPMENT. You'd be surprised how many times horses work poorly, even turn silly in their behavior, because of some irritation from a bridle that may have one bit strap twisted causing tight pressure on one side of the mouth. Or the saddle blanket has a kink that is rubbing against his back. Or perhaps not enough padding is under the saddle and your weight is cutting into the horse.

If the equipment is satisfactory and comfortable for the horse, and he has rarely been shiftless in working his routine, then return him to his stall for an hour or two and try again later. Horses, too, have their off days. Be sympathetic to this possibility. The idea of always making a horse do what you want, when you want, and not giving up until he obeys your royal command, is harsh and frequently unnecessary.

Besides, continual fighting with your horse every time you are in the saddle puts him on the defensive. He can hardly think of training or routine work if he is worried about his well-being. And as I have said before, you can bet your last money the horse's well-being is always foremost in his mind.

Daily routine training is the best course for teaching a horse because, again, repetition is important to his learning. But watch for *excessiveness* in that routine. Tests have shown that spacing new work, say every other day, with routine work the other days, allows the horse to learn more rapidly than pursuing daily routines on a prolonged basis. In other words, spacing the lessons between known work and a ride outside the training area into the woods or hills or desert—wherever you happen to live—seems to promote better retentiveness in the horse's mind. It reduces, also, the possibility of the horse becoming stale or belligerent.

These past paragraphs have been building toward the idea that you must develop the *feel* in arranging training schedules and sizing up your horse in order to avoid punishment and fights. This way you keep him interested in his work. Another side of this feel is learning when he is taking advantage of you and is becoming a slacker. If this trend is allowed to continue, and you do not punish accordingly, be assured he will put up a good scrap to retain these newly won habits that benefit him.

If the horse is definitely testing you, punishment is mandatory. The punishment must not be put off, but administered immediately after the disobedience. Then he will realize what he is being punished for. Extended punishment, keep in mind, only makes a horse feel you are fighting him and, justifiably, he feels he must fight back.

Above all, training is a matter of developing certain habits and manners for horses to perform. Good habits are those developed to the trainer's satisfaction. Bad habits are not. Firm and immediate punishment minimizes bad habits.

Confused? Don't be. Intellectually, you are now, at least, aware of punishment-persuasion—how it works, some of its subtleties, the *feel* involved. You are now only fifty percent in the dark (since you still have to try it out for yourself), but that's better than being totally in the dark. I have seen a good many amateurs who, after two weeks of good training with their horses, suddenly become depressed because their horses were turning sour and were fighting them. They blamed themselves as being bad trainers. But once they were enlightened on some of these matters I've discussed—like punishing when the horse is testing, or allowing the horse a respite from training routine—their horses responded again with interest and their own confidence was restored. It wasn't their lack of talent that caused the problem so much as a failure to interpret various situations and learn how to correct them.

To conclude this chapter, let's discuss something pleasant—rewards. Just as with corrections, rewards should be given immediately. After a horse has successfully accomplished a request, reassure him with a pat and friendly verbal praise. This lets him know he has responded correctly and has pleased you. He is keen to sense enthusiasm in the human voice, just as he is quick to grasp reprimands, both verbal and physical. Correction, when necessary and properly given, sharpens the horse and his respect for you. Praise, when deserved, builds his confidence.

CHAPTER

5

GROUND TRAINING I

This is a good time to sum up a few key ideas we have been discussing before starting with training directions.

I hope I have instilled the idea that training is an applied skill, just as painting and sculpting are. And regardless of how much one may read on the subject of horse training (or painting and sculpting), skill can be developed only through actual practice. You must undertake training first-hand before you can benefit from book ideas. (I'd like to believe this book will be granted a few exceptions, since it presents theory and background filtered for use in practical learning.) Afterwards, a combination of practice and theory will help streamline your skills. But just as painters or sculptors develop a feel for their materials—brushes, oils and clay—so does a horseman improve the basis for his skills through understanding the nature of the horse and its response to stimuli.

The horse, therefore, is the trainer's clay. How well the horse trains mirrors the trainer's understanding of the horse's mind and his thinking patterns. We have seen that the horse is not too intelligent, or endowed with much reasoning power. He cannot think as you do, so you must learn to think as the horse does, and apply training that best harmonizes with the horse's habit-like nature and his particular personality profile. Firmness and exactness in training, through punishment-persuasion, establishes the limits of the habits (that is, what you expect of the horse), and repetition develops the habits into trained responses.

Also, if you are a novice, a horse with a pleasant disposition—not overexcitable or excessively sluggish—is preferred for student training. This type of horse is easier to manage and will even allow margins for error in its training.

I want to add, now, another of those few absolutes in the training of horses. It is a reflection of the trainer who has polished his or her skills. It is this: *A good horseman uses the simplest methods and the simplest equipment, but uses them superlatively well.*

This is the true meaning, and result, of learning from experience, and by thinking! You may never, therefore, have to be in awe, or fooled, by the braggart who boasts of twenty years of experience, and yet has a multitude of bits and gimmicks and is tough with his horses. This sort of individual has not learned through experience. In essence, he has had about one year's experience twenty times over. He has not grown. I mention this particular criticism because novices invariably look to the experienced horseman for advice and observation. Fine. But there are as many poor horsemen about as there are accomplished ones. Learn to distinguish the one who can help you grow.

The one way to grow is to accept challenges. Whenever you have a training problem with your horse (and it happens to all of us), don't turn immediately to a stronger bit, a stouter whip, a gimmick, or whatever cure-all is in vogue on the horse equipment market. You are not really solving your problem (exceptions will be discussed in a later chapter), and may be intensifying it. If you have a problem, stop, or get off the horse, and analyze the trouble. Confront it right there, because people who have training problems also have horses who have people problems. And you, not your horse, must work out a solution which is acceptable to the horse, if it is to be properly trained.

Neither should you overlook the latent learning of horses. Often one has the inkling that the horse isn't grasping the training aim; that the time lapse seems excessive for the demand being made upon the horse. But patience is also a tool which, when used superlatively well, allows a horse sufficient time to grasp a lesson. One training session may be all that is necessary. Possibly seven sessions may be required over a week's time. *A horse needs time to learn, and a trainer must have the self-discipline to allow his horse ample time to absorb a lesson.*

Too frequently, trainers who believe they aren't being persuasive in one training lesson switch to another. This usually changes the technique or patterns they previously followed, often just when the horse, through latent learning, was beginning to understand the first aim of the trainer. Now, the horse can only become confused.

Self-discipline, along with an immediate training aim, and the patience to allow the horse a chance to learn—often through latent learning—prevents a number of training problems ever developing.

In the last chapter about punishment-persuasion I said that you should arrange your training, or a break from training, to avoid circumstances which might require punishing unnecessarily. An additional way to avoid an overburden of training problems while you are learning is through ground training the horse.

Many basics can be taught from the ground while mentally conditioning a young horse to a working routine without stress or strain. (Actually, any horse, young or not so young, green, or literally calloused from all sorts of handling, can benefit from ground training.) It is a way of establishing rapport and developing the essence of *feel* which, as I say over and over, is the basis for the refining of training skills.

A novice who attempts to train from the saddle is setting up two strikes against himself. Not only does he have the challenge of controlling the training itself, but also (unless he is an excellent rider) the problem of not interfering with training through poor seat and hands.

It is also true that—human nature being what it is—there is too much temptation to work the reins in a heavy fashion. This distracts the horse from his training. He is more concerned about what is happening to his mouth. Ground training not only permits a novice less worry about maintaining control, but allows the best opportunity to understand the effects of punishment-persuasion.

Furthermore, training horses from the saddle at two years of age, even three, is an almost certain invitation to splints, ringbone, curbed hocks and a host of other leg ailments that plague the horse. And yet, riding young horses, even though these hazards are known, is almost invariably compromised by a creeping eagerness to mount and try the horse "just a little bit." Before long, many horses are deep into training despite the rider's self-promise to "take it easy" until the animal to be trained has some age behind him.

This white lie begins with a slight attempt to collect, a slight attempt to neck-rein or try a pivot, or a sliding stop or a low jump. And since the horse usually performs quite nicely in those first lessons we compliment ourselves on some clever handling or on the horse's unusual intelligence. We are encouraged to continue, and frequently we end in sorrow.

Granted, young horses do learn rapidly. Little else has been taught them and their minds are not filled with cues and responses. Besides, young horses are anxious to please and, for some, their confidence hasn't been corroded by mismanagement.

I'll admit that some professionals do a creditable job working young horses. Some do not. But almost all amateurs find that their efforts result in confused, sour horses because of demands pushed too rapidly. And although setbacks in training can, fortunately, be corrected with time, little can alter any leg injuries incurred. These can be permanent or intermittent handicaps, all of which returns us to ground training.

For the initial ground training—training other than lunging—you will need a riding crop about 25 inches long. Play with it. Wiggle it around in your fingers. Twirl it like a baton. Get the feel of it, particularly in your left hand. Develop the knack, through wrist and finger action, of reversing the tip end of the whip, from pointing in back of you to pointing in front. When the whip is held with the tip pointing down and behind you, your hand should grasp the top of the whip as you would hold onto a rope you were climbing. When, by finger and wrist movement, you manipulate the whip so the top of the whip turns in your hand and the tip is pointing forward, your hand should be grasping it as if you were holding a fishing rod. As I've said, it's a knack which merely takes a little practice. Yet you must learn to reverse whip positions in a smooth, quick motion or your awkwardness will only interfere with the training procedure.

Our aim in this first set of lessons is to teach a horse to walk, trot, stop and stand on command. You say, "My horse already does that." Maybe so. But it must be taught precisely so the horse responds to verbal cues, respects the whip, does not anticipate, and performs a walk, trot and a halt with alertness, briskness and obedience. And these disciplines must be taught thoroughly so they can be carried, later, into lunging and training from the saddle.

We begin.

Your horse, haltered just loose enough so a pull on the shank will bring pressure from the noseband, is placed alongside a fence or building—preferably a long straight-away to allow starts and stops without having to reverse direction too frequently.

Position your horse against the barrier while you stand just about at its left shoulder. The halter shank is in your right hand, arranged so the coils of the shank (it should be about three feet long) hang loosely and fairly long. Tight coils will only catch your hand too quickly if the horse should pull back. Allow the coils to rest over your second finger while that part of the shank that attaches to the halter is grasped between the thumb and forefinger about six inches from the halter ring.

Vibrate the halter slightly to be positive you have the horse's attention. (Incidentally, work away from other horses whenever possible.)

Your whip should be hanging down alongside your left leg, tip pointing slightly to the rear. In a normal voice say, "alk." (Drop the *w*. This consonant has a long sound and will be confused by the horse when you say, "whoa.") As you command "alk," turn your wrist so that the tip of the whip strikes at the horse's barrel, about where a leg aid would touch if you were mounted, and walk on.

I cannot tell you precisely how much whip pressure you must use. It should not be the full force of your wrist and arm action, but neither so slight that the horse is merely tickled and he flips his tail as if to chase a fly. It must be firm. The horse must know he has been stung.

Now your horse might step out without fuss. This is not likely. What can happen is that the horse may lunge forward when he feels the whip. Without becoming excited yourself (remember the *as if* game), merely calm him down while walking. Of course, you should have a fairly good hold on your lead shank so it is not pulled easily out of your hand. But if it is, and he turns toward you when you have checked him with the shank, straighten him out, gather your coil quickly, and, using your voice cue, walk on.

Possibly the horse will pull back when he feels the whip. When he does, you will loosen the first coil, because of its position in your hand. That's okay. In that moment, your hand will have tightened on the remaining coils which should stop the horse when he feels the halter tighten. Again, straighten him out. And this time try walking ahead first, and the second the horse follows, apply the cues.

A horse that steps back is more of a problem than one that lunges forward. If you find yourself confronted with a horse stepping back again and again, be careful that you are not setting up a habit. Change the pattern. Work him from a corner of a fence line so he can't step back on you.

Once you have the horse walking don't allow him to lag. His head and neck should precede you while you hold a position even with his shoulder. If he lags, say, "alk," and use the whip.

After your horse has walked about a dozen strides— that is, is walking energetically—you are ready to teach the second command, "whoa."

Again, coordinate the use of the whip and voice. This

A well-mannered horse and a young lady who has learned training manners and the principles of disciplining her horse.

Proper placement of whip cue. Horses respond differently to whip contact in the first lessons of training.

is essential. So is timing. As I said, the horse should be walking with impulsion. Let the whip drop from its position behind you, bring it past your leg while your hand switches position on the handle so it is held like a fishing pole and bring it up smartly and strike the horse across the chest, commanding "whoa" in a firm, slightly louder tone than "alk" and halt yourself while taking a backward tug on the halter shank. Don't yell out "whoa." You might frighten the horse so he's ready to jump out of his halter. The command must be uttered strongly, but not loudly.

Your horse will probably stop square in his tracks. If he does, cease all pressures. Lower the whip quickly and rub the bottom part of his neck with your knuckles.

If your horse, when feeling the whip, suddenly rushes backward, merely hold on with a steady pressure. Strongly repeat "whoa" until he stops. Neither pet him nor punish him in these instances, but merely start again.

As I have indicated, it is unlikely that the walking out or the halt will come off smoothly the first few times. Yet it might. But if it doesn't, don't become upset. This is what training is about. After all, if the horse performed everything asked of him without a fuss, there would be no need for instructions.

Remember the ideal you are training for:

1. The horse to stand alertly.
2. The horse to precede you when you say "alk," immediately followed by the whip cue as you yourself step forward.

The whip carelessly applied . . . and the result.

Overleaf: Left, teaching whoa *requires the whip to be brought smartly against the horse's chest.*

Right, the reaction of a young horse when the cue for whoa *was first applied.*

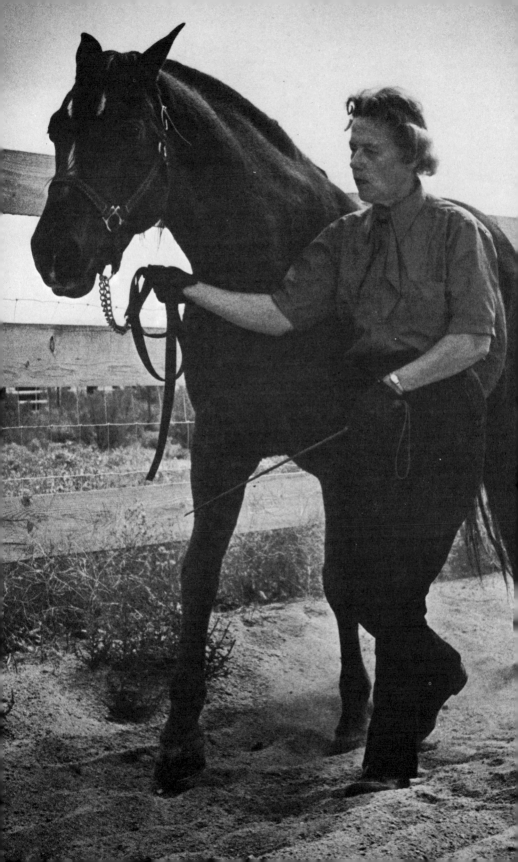

3. The horse not to lag back. (If he does, repeat the cues.)
4. The horse to stop squarely when you apply the whip and voice cues and halt yourself.

The moment he does these movements with some correctness reward him by rubbing your knuckles against the bottom of his neck.

Vary the number of strides you walk the horse before calling for a halt. Otherwise, he will begin anticipating stopping if, say, at every five strides you regularly command the halt.

Two more points to remember: Don't swing your whip out in a swooping arc. Your horse can see fairly well to the side and you can spook him before the whip has even touched his body. I can't repeat enough that you must develop a dexterous handling of the whip from back to front so it strikes quickly and accurately—and with no loss of motion.

Secondly, your body positions are important and must remain consistent. When you stop your horse squarely, you, too, stand squarely facing the front. Don't turn to face him or turn away. As I said, you can pet him, without moving your body excessively, by rubbing the knuckles of your halter hand against his neck. These body positions will count when you get to lunging. Plus, they will also prove to be of benefit in halter and showmanship classes, as we will soon see.

All right, the horse has halted. Now stand for a few moments. After another halt stand for one minute, then revert to a moment's halt, or one of half a minute, at succeeding halts. If he should move, strike him hard with the whip and repeat the verbal command. Don't forget, you are teaching not only commands, but discipline too. So don't slack off. "Whoa" to the horse must mean to stop and stand.

It is difficult to say just how long it will take the horse

to learn these commands. In fact, if you should ask this question, you are only betraying some form of impatience. It takes as long as it takes. Some horses have learned in a few lessons of ten minutes each. Others have required much more patient work.

The lessons should be frequent, in any case, with rest periods in between. Ten minutes per session is approximate. But more important, *until you are sure* the horse is responding to the verbal commands, use both voice and whip cues. Of course, if your horse is responding nicely, lessen the use or the intensity of the whip. You don't want to sour him.

On the other hand, the moment he does not obey, get after him. Training is directing a behavior pattern, and you can only impress the pattern on the horse by correcting his disobedience and rewarding compliance by ceasing the use of the whip and giving him a pat. No training accomplishment comes to you in full blossom with the first cue. You work for it by building it increment by increment.

Let's say you have your horse walking out nicely and stopping in quick response to the cues. Now you may feel that as you say, "alk," the horse is stepping out on the verbal command. But watch yourself. What he is probably doing is following your body motion as you walk out, or the whip cue. Here is how you test him. Say, "alk," but do not move yourself in that instant. If he is picking up the word cue he will take a step or two himself (and you then immediately take up the pace yourself). If he doesn't move out, then follow quickly with the whip cue.

Also, with the stop, you must test to see if he is stopping because you have stopped or is actually obeying the voice cue. When you are ready to stop, command "whoa" as you take another step yourself. If he is taking the word cue, he will stop. If he still hasn't associated the word with halting, he will still be following your body motion. Of course, immediately strike with the whip and command, "whoa." Test these reactions, and, if necessary, start intensifying the voice-whip association with stronger whip use.

Now a word of caution on the halting part of training. Keep a keen eye on him when he stops. What I mean is that, usually, because the cue is much firmer for the stop, the horse learns this far quicker than the verbal command to walk. So don't keep striking at him once he has picked up the word cue. After a half dozen uses of the whip for the halt, try it once without the whip (unless you are positive he is not listening at all). If he is obeying the voice, fine; but every fourth or fifth stop use the whip just to make sure he isn't forgetting.

Thus far you have worked your horse at the walk and the halt. You know how to test to see if the horse is learning the verbal cue. Assuming he has learned your voice commands, and can therefore perform on verbal indications and also on your body motions, and that his walk is energetic and his halts prompt, let's go a step further.

You have halted and are standing beside your horse. Now, in an easy motion, transfer the lead shank into your left hand and the whip to your right, gripping it as you would a rope. Hold it horizontally at about waist level.

Turn toward the horse, then step back so you are facing him straight on. At the same time say, "whoa, whoa." If the horse moves by trying to follow you, correct immediately while commanding, "whoa." Your whip is in its best position for a rapid correction.

What you are teaching your horse is to stand *whenever you face him no matter where you stand or move*. (Ever see halter classes where horses are jumping or fidgeting all around the length of a halter shank?)

This horse is walking out nicely on verbal command. Note that the whip is held in a down or neutral position while the horse walks out energetically. If the horse should fall behind the handler's pace, whip and voice cues are immediately brought into effect.

When you return to your horse's side, merely walk forward to his shoulder area, switch whip and lead shank hands, and then turn about so you and your horse are ready to move forward.

Practice this, and if the horse is responding with obedience, extend the distance between you and the horse until you can go out to the end of the shank with the horse standing obediently.

Once your horse is confirmed to stand, you can teach him to come to you on a specific cue. Turn your back to him and, looking over your shoulder to him, say "here" and pull him to you with the halter shank.

Encourage the horse to come to you and stop when you are at about his shoulder area.

These lessons are usually learned quickly by a horse. But don't forget: *Do not go to an advanced step of training until the horse is confirmed in the previous step.* I assure you that if the basic step is not confirmed in the horse, confusion by the horse will be evident when you attempt an additional training step. What's more, you will not have trained the horse in either step and possibly will have compounded training problems.

After you have taught your horse to stand to the full length of the shank (if properly confirmed, you should be able to go the length of a lunging line and your horse will stand) and he comes to you only when you turn your back and command "here," start working these same lessons away from the fence or whatever boundary you have been using.

Additionally, you now want to be able to walk to the left or right of your horse as he stands. This is simple enough.

Teaching the horse to stand attentively. The handler holds the whip in front of her chest. Once this lesson is confirmed, the horse is worked away from the fence.

Standing a few feet in front of him, take three or four steps to your right, return to center and take a few steps to your left. Your horse might attempt to follow, so be ready to correct. Following a few short lessons, take more steps left and right until you can move about forty-five degrees to your horse either way. Then, repeat this procedure with a longer length of lead shank between you and your horse.

One additional item remains to be learned by the horse while at halter: trotting. Again, if your preparation has been correct, teaching a strong trot at halter is not difficult.

Walk your horse along the fence. Be sure it is a lively pace. Then, using your whip in a quick tap-tap fashion, increase the pace of your walk and command in a sing-song way, "*ttrrott!*" and assume an easy running motion yourself. All this "movement" is generally exciting for the horse, and just a little bit more encouragement with the whip and voice entices him to trot on.

Stopping from the trot follows the same procedure used at the walk. But in the case of the trot, be alert to the horse anticipating the stop, and change the pattern of the number of strides you work with. In fact, fool him occasionally. Trot out two or three strides and then call for a halt. Then six or eight strides, then back to five, and so on.

Once your horse responds readily and obediently, you have a horse trained in basic disciplines. He walks, trots, stands and comes to you on command. He understands verbal as well as body cues.

You, meanwhile, will have learned about horse behavior and understand more fully the punishment-persuasion technique. Consequently, a *feel* and rapport will provide you with an added sense of confidence.

A nice strong trot is easily obtained if work at the walk is thoroughly understood by the horse. Note that the horse is not lagging behind the handler. Note also the whip position when the horse is performing satisfactorily.

There are some practical benefits you can now use at a show, either in halter classes or showmanship classes (if you happen to be in the correct age bracket for the latter class). Let me illustrate what points you can garner (especially in showmanship classes) with your *trained* horse as compared to what is frequently seen in the show arena.

The judge comes to an entrant who is standing at the horse's head and holding the shank about one inch away from the halter. The horse is also probably half asleep, or perhaps jumping about with little control. The judge looks at the horse from the front and the handler hardly moves to give the judge a good look at his or her horse. Or the handler stands at the horse's side and blocks the judge's view there too. What a judge would like to say to the contestant—and some do—is, "I can't judge your horse if you don't allow me to see him."

But with your horse, now trained as he is, you can stand away or to the side and never block a judge's view. Moreover, you can encourage him to alertness when the judge is in your immediate area and still have your animal stand still.

Also, you will have the advantage when the judge asks you to trot out your horse. You've probably seen instances when the handler immediately starts a trot himself and the horse, taken by surprise, jerks back, or merely walks while the handler is practically pulling the horse's head off. What you can do is walk two strides, then command, "*ttrrott,*" and both of you step out. You may not win your class, but your judge will notice and appreciate your horse-handling techniques.

Practice these elementary lessons on as many horses as you can muster. Often, friends will allow you to work their horses if you have shown that you can improve their discipline and level of training. A variety of horses presents a variety of experience.

6

GROUND TRAINING II

The disciplines that you have taught your horse in basic ground training are the foundation for training on the lunge line. If your preparation has been faulty, you will be told through your horse in this next stage of training. He will display uncertainty, perhaps a tinge of fear, and an inability to respond properly on the lunge. He will not be unlike the child who begins school in the third grade without the benefits of the first and second grades. You can imagine the disadvantages. This analogy holds true also when training a horse and leads to a truism that bears repeating: *Never advance a horse's training until it is confirmed in the previous lesson.* Otherwise, setbacks are inevitable.

If your preliminary work has been correct, further training advances with considerably more ease and, in the long run, faster.

By taking your time in basic training, you will have, through punishment-persuasion techniques, let your horse know what is expected of him. And rewards, in gentle pats, soothing words, and varying training routines, assist the training process. Combine these and you produce a discipline in your horse that is a willing submission. Of course, all this implies that you are consistent in your method.

Now we arrive at the second stage of ground training—lunging. Please dismiss from your mind what you are likely to see ninety percent of the time being passed off as lunging: a horse running around in a circle, usually at full speed and usually without any control other than the handler's leaning back on the lunge line with the weight of his body.

Correct lunging is almost a lost art, a victim, one might say, of the *rush* and *quick results* syndrome that too frequently characterizes the American character. Too bad, really, for correct lunging can reflect a delicate harmony between man and horse, a satisfying experience of mutual trust and understanding between horse and handler.

To observe proper lunging is a pleasure. It is even more pleasing if you are at the end of the lunge line directing the horse to walk, trot and canter with lightness and obedience and without pulling. The sensation conveys much of the sense of *feel* and *rapport* between you and your horse.

Let's not overlook the practical aspects either. Lunging is an excellent method for increasing the horse's discipline and his proficiency at the gaits. It is especially useful in developing the horse's balance, pace and rhythm. Pardon me if I sound carried away, but I want to make you aware what lunging's potential is and, hopefully, make you dissatisfied with half-efforts and half-results.

I must caution, however, that since you will be working further away from your horse, perhaps twenty-five to thirty feet at the end of the lunge line, it should be obvious that control is minimal. Therefore, *lunging requires that each stage be fixed in the horse's mind before an advanced stage of lunging commences.* And just as proficiency with a riding crop was essential for teaching at halter training, lunging requires skill with a lunge whip (about a five-foot stock and five-foot lash). So play with this whip. Learn to use it. Toss the lash out and bring it back to you without wrapping yourself up in it. Develop the ability to crack it smartly. When you can gauge the whip and send the lash out and merely touch the horse with the tip, you can accept yourself as proficient.

What can a horse be taught on the lunge?

The gaits, of course. But more important, controlling the tempo and developing extended work at the gaits (which is not the same as *rushing* the gaits), collecting, and changing directions through the middle of the circle. The horse is made supple and wind capacity is improved. Obedience is deeply ingrained. Your horse will understand you better, as well as the concept of training, and you will understand horses and their training more perceptively.

I'll be frank. Much of what I admire in lunging is really an end in itself. Other than the basics, one need not take one's horse into advanced work on the lunge, but I enjoy advanced lunging because it tests me. I enjoy the challenge of having only a length of lunge line between me and the horse and communicating by voice, body and lunge whip positions the responses I want from the horse. I am, actually, testing myself. And while I have at times had horses that did not respond as I would have wished (and my ego suffered), others have performed to a degree that made me proud to display the horses in lunging demonstrations.

Yet I will not delve here into advanced lunging techniques. So much counts in the personal rapport between you and your horse that my set of instructions will not be sufficient for you. It is a personalized harmony, but one you can reach if you perfect the basics.

For the first few lessons, we begin with a plain halter, a riding crop (or a buggy whip with no lash) and an extra long halter shank. You could begin with a regular lunge line, with most of the coils hanging loose (large loops, please), but it could be a bit cumbersome since we will be working at close quarters with the horse in the first lesson.

The first idea to teach the horse is to walk around you in about a five- to ten-foot circle. A small enclosure is preferable, but if one is not available, then you must make use of what is readily handy. A fence corner is excellent, but even an open area will suffice. Mainly, in these first few lessons, be certain that your horse is calm. What I mean is don't attempt this work if the horse has been stabled for three days without excercise and is full of vigor. Or if other horses are nearby and enticing your horse to give his attention to them and not you. Also, working your horse before he has eaten, particularly if his stablemates are enjoying their morning grain, diverts his attention. These are small items, but only in the sense that they are easily overlooked. They can (no matter what the training) erect strong barriers between you and your horse. So, calmness in your horse and minimal distractions are prime requirements.

Assuming you have an area to work your horse, place his offside next to a fence or side of a building. We will begin working the horse to the left, counterclockwise, since that direction tends to be easiest for the horse. And as he is already versed in the commands to walk, halt and stand, you should have no problem positioning yourself in a line about five feet from his shoulder.

You will recall in the last chapter that I stressed how body positions serve as cues to your horse. Lunging requires even more careful attention to your positions, and let me repeat, the horse will assimilate these positions readily and associate them with his movements on the lunge. Thus you must be conscious of your movements, so don't become careless with them.

A neutral position is on a line from the horse's shoulder to yourself. The bodily cue to move forward is indicated by stepping toward the horse's flank. Halting is indicated by stepping to a point in line with the horse's eye. Finally, in cueing the horse to reverse through the middle of the circle you must cross in front of him. Establish these basic cues correctly at the walk and you will find training at the trot and canter an almost automatic response by the horse.

Now we return to our horse standing with his off-side alongside a fence or building wall and you in line about five feet from his shoulder. Step about two paces toward his flank, command easily, "alk," and point the whip at his gaskin area.

I wish I could say your horse will walk out properly on the lunge. Maybe he will. More likely you will have to tap him with the whip and perhaps you may have to move another pace or two toward his rear. Possibly your horse will try and turn into you. So you may have to quickly point the whip toward his nose to straighten him out. At that moment he may want to stop and you will have to again move toward his rear.

As you can see, you may have to be as nimble as Fred Astaire. But do not hop with lightning speed back and forth. That will only excite and confuse the horse. *Feel out the procedure.* Mainly, get him walking. Once you do, keep encouraging him with the verbal command while maintaining your body position in an area to the rear of his shoulder. But stay calm and moderate your voice command at the same level or pitch you used in the previous ground work at halter.

Keep your horse moving around you until he begins to understand your wishes. Watch your body position and your position at the whip. To stop your horse wait until he is turning into a position parallel to the fence, then step forward until you are in line with his eye and command, "whoa." At the same time, position your riding crop just in front of his chest. Let him stand a moment, then go over and pet him.

Halting the horse alongside a fence barrier not only aids your control, but in addition teaches him to stop straight. Establishing this habit will prevent, later, the inclination of the horse to turn in toward the circle and face you.

You will note how you have used past established cues in conjunction with newer cues. Your horse will also have noted them, and fixed in his mind the newer cues with a different set of responses. Yet he can assimilate these newer responses only because of the basic responses you have taught him at halter.

Starting a horse to lunge begins with a continuation of walking along the fence. Here the handler is urging the horse to the verbal command "alk" ("walk" without the w). Notice the whip at neutral position but ready to encourage the horse if he should hesitate. Note, too, the horse's look of attention to the handler's verbal command.

After the horse has learned to walk around the handler, it is also instructed to obey the command of "whoa." The camera has caught this moment as the handler steps toward the front of the horse and commands "whoa."

After the horse understands the idea of walking around the handler, the same procedure is executed away from the fence. Note handler's use of the whip to encourage the horse.

Possibly another approach may work better for you and your horse. You can begin walking with him as you did in the basic ground work. Then slip the halter shank from your right hand to your left, and keeping up your verbal command, "alk," step back while tapping lightly with your whip on the horse's flank and starting the horse to circle. If you can do this smoothly you might start your horse out on the lunge in this manner. I prefer the first approach and have had more success with it, but you must find your own.

The entire procedure might not go well at first, but if you stick with it, the horse will begin to get the idea. You may have to constantly reposition him against the fence and start again and again because the horse insists on turning into you. And you may have to strike him on the shoulder with the whip if it appears to you he is starting up a habit of turning in. But don't lose your temper. Calmness and repetition will win out.

All right. Now you have your horse moving out on a small circle and he will stop on command and stand. If you get five good starts and stops, with your horse walking around you two or three times between starts and stops, he has the idea.

Now you must teach him the same procedure going clockwise. You begin just as you did previously, but now you position the horse with his nearside next to the fence. However, expect a bit of stiffness and hesitancy from the horse. As I mentioned in a previous chapter, working a horse from his offside is a bit uncomfortable and awkward for him. It's our own fault, since we work our horses from the nearside and tend to make them left-handed. If you keep in mind how awkward it is to throw a ball or write with the hand that is unnatural for you, you will understand the unhandiness a horse also experiences when worked from his offside. (A good reason, by the way, for also teaching a horse to lead from his offside and for giving as much casual attention to that side as his nearside.)

Once you have your horse working from both sides of the lunge line—and you probably should work him more to the right to develop suppleness—encourage him to walk further out on the line. Actually, you give that impression to the horse. When you are ready for this phase, exchange your halter shank for a lunge line and begin working the horse in the middle of the arena.

As your horse walks out, allow a couple of loops of the lunge line to slip from your hand and step back to take up the slack, all the while, encouraging the horse with the verbal "alk" commands. He will be wondering what you are doing and may try to come into you, or stop. Repeating "alk" keeps his attention on the command (he can't think of two things at once). Still, you may have to move in, and with your whip (with a lash) either flip the lash toward his muzzle, if he does step in, or encourage him to move on by gently swinging the lash at his rump. Often it is not necessary to touch the horse with the lash, but just let him see it. This usually suffices. But once again, you must feel out your own situation, and perhaps a slight touch of the lash may be necessary. Sometimes even a sharp crack.

Also, from the beginning lessons on the lunge line, keep a *slight pressure* on the line; not enough to force the horse to feel his head is being turned into you, but just enough so there is only the lightest amount of slack. The reason for this is to condition the horse to want to feel a slight pressure. Thus, it allows him to know how far out he is to work on the lunge line. As your work progresses, you will find that when you give slack, instead of your having to step back to take up the slack, the horse will expand his circle to make up for the lack of feeling on the lunge line. Do not become too concerned about this; you will find that the horse himself will probably search for some pressure on the lunge line as you encourage him to enlarge his circle.

Let me back up a moment and bring in a few other points:

1. Always wear gloves when lunging your horse. There will be times when your horse will suddenly, from exuberance or from being frightened, run pell-mell. Unless you have gloves you may feel fire in your hands from friction burns. You know as well as I do that if a horse decides to move out he can be hard to stop.

2. Keep control over the loops of the lunge line. Learn to hold large loops across your index finger. If your horse should suddenly bolt you would lose only a few loops until you are able to check him. Small loops wrapped around your hand would be the same as if your horse had lassoed you. They would tighten immediately if he bolted and you could get a wrenched hand, not to mention being dragged.

3. If your horse should display a sudden burst of speed, stay calm. Don't start shouting "whoa" when he is in that state. He probably won't listen. Just start talking in easy tones to him while looping in the lunge line and decreasing the size of his circle. Eventually he will come to a whirling stop. Let him relax a few minutes to calm him down. Then start again.

4. Watch your whip positions. If your horse is moving out on the lunge in the prescribed manner, keep your whip pointing downward. Lift it only to indicate a cue or encouragement to him. *Remember, he knows where the whip is all the time, even if you don't.* And if you are carelessly flipping it here and there the horse is not going to be concentrating on what you are trying to teach him.

5. Even the best trainer is occasionally going to lose control over his lunge line and get it wrapped around the horse's leg or between his legs; or the horse will smell along the ground and step over the lunge and get it between his legs. In the event this happens, give slack immediately and command "whoa" (calmly, please!). If he stops, fine. However, some horses, when feeling a lunge line tightening on their legs, immediately panic. If you can hold on, he might just stop. Others can move so fast and with so much power that you lose the lunge line and away

Continuing the lunging process, the handler is now using a regular
lunge line and lunging whip. The horse is encouraged into a wider
circular pattern.

they go! Either they eventually stop, or the line breaks at the halter snap, or they trip themselves and extricate themselves another way.

Any of the above possibilities can be minimized by repeating two points already mentioned: watch your slack on the lunge line. Remember, a horse can step over the lunge line in a second. Also, do not go into trotting and cantering on the lunge line until the horse is absolutely confirmed at the walk. This is not only "training sense," but a sensible procedure for yourself until you can work a lunge line and whip and manage your positions with ease.

Assuming these conditions prevail and your horse can walk out on the lunge line in either direction at least twenty feet, and will stop on command (preferably straight and not turning into you, although if he does there is little you can now do to correct, so don't be concerned), it is time to teach him to trot.

He already knows the command *"ttrrott,"* so you merely have to let him walk about ten feet out on the lunge line and then cue him verbally and flip the whip and touch his rump. The intensity of the whip cue depends on your horse. Only you know him and how much encouragement he needs. Nonetheless, you should have little difficulty in encouraging the horse to trot. Allow him to trot around you a few times. Do not encourage speed; just a quiet trot. Then, using a few easy tugs on the lunge, use your verbal command to make him walk. Some horses respond immediately and drop into a walk. Others may have to be brought to a walk by decreasing the circle while you continuously command, "alk." When the horse drops into a walk (don't let him halt), let him walk about ten feet, then stop and pet him. Establish this pattern thoroughly until your horse will go from a walk to a trot and a trot to a walk without any shortening of the lunge line. Don't forget the slight trembling of the lunge line before calling for a decrease in a gait. This is an attention-getter prior to the command. Granted, with sufficient practice and consistency, a horse will work from the verbal commands. But remember, the ideas in this book are intended to reveal to you also the "little ways" one communicates with horses— voice, body positions, physical contacts—and to show how very keen are the horse's observations in reading your messages.

Once your horse understands the mechanics of lunging, you must next encourage him to extend his walk and trot. Remember, any exercise which develops physical improvement in suppleness and balance requires an effort beyond the horse's normal pace. After you are certain that your horse can walk and trot, with obedience to your commands and in both directions to the end of the lunge line (twenty to thirty feet), you can start to teach more control over the gaits.

Starting with the walk, let your horse walk his normal stride about ten feet out on the lunge. Then, using the whip lash near or at the horse's hind legs (depending on which gets the results) and uttering a series of "alk" commands, encourage him to increase his stride. The key word here is *encourage*. That's about all you can do. Your horse might break into a trot, but bring him back to a walk and immediately encourage him, with voice and whip, to increase his stride. Assuming a body position a bit further toward his rear is an encouraging stimulus.

The same procedure is used for the trot. But be sure you let out enough lunge line, as the horse needs a wider turning radius.

Don't ask for too much extension too quickly. What you want to accomplish, gradually, is the ability of your horse to increase his stride. Learn to detect when the increase indicates that your horse is actually working— that is, putting forth an effort—and be content with that degree. Don't keep pushing him merely for more speed simply because that indicates to you that you're able to encourage the horse to walk or trot rapidly. A longer stride, not quicker steps, is what your eye should measure.

With the horse trotting on a large circle and you making "encouraging" efforts for him to extend his stride, he likely will break into a canter. Immediately cease the motions you were using to increase the stride. Gradually fish-in the lunge line to decrease the size of the circle while calling out to the horse to "ttrrott." Once the horse drops back into a trot, allow him to go quietly along. *But notice the point where he drops from the canter to the trot. It is this point which is probably the horse's best effort at the extended trot.* When you again encourage him to extend the pace, don't let your efforts carry your horse beyond that point. In other words, read his potential, and don't ask for more than that particular horse can offer. Of course, with continuous exercise, say over a period of five weeks, he probably could give a little more. Ask yourself, however, if "more" is necessary. If your horse can perform his ordinary trot and carry it to a strong extension, that is satisfaction enough and the particular idea—for the horse and yourself—has been taught.

Another thing to work at with the trot is its collected form. To slow your horse down while maintaining energy in the stride, begin by slowly decreasing the size of the circle. Yet encourage your horse to impulsion. If you're gentle, you can have your horse perform a collected trot in a fifteen-foot radius. You should be able to sense, by now, that the idea is to give and take with smoothness: slowing the horse with the lunge while encouraging him by voice, whip position (near his hind legs to urge him on if his stride begins to fall apart) and your own position are the fine touches that increase even your sense of *feel* in training horses.

Do not fool yourself, though, with a horse that is essentially a deadbeat. Frankly, if your horse tends to be lazy, there is little use expanding effort teaching it to collect on the lunge line. A horse with some spirit will respond more easily. So, if your horse is not endowed with a fair amount of natural vitality, content yourself with teaching him his normal walk and trot on the lunge line.

The canter is the next gait to develop. Presumably, you will have waited until your horse walks and trots in both directions, halts straight and—if he shows the potential—can extend and collect the two gaits with a fair amount of pluck. Asking for the canter, therefore, is no problem at all. I begin by letting the horse trot out to the end of the lunge line, but positioning myself so that he will pass alongside a fence line on his circular tour. As he trots into the fence line (clockwise), I sort of hunch over at the shoulder, rush in toward his flank, crack the whip, and bellow in a guttural tone, "CANTER!"

Cueing him as he leads into the fence is to insure he picks up his proper lead. If you don't have a natural barrier, be certain when you command the canter that the lunge line is slack. A tight hold would force the horse to strike off on the outside lead since his head is drawn in toward the inside of the circle. I emphasize the whip crack and the coming toward him to excite him into the canter because the verbal command is new to him. More often than not, my horses will leap into a canter, rather wildly I'll admit, but they have associated the verbal command with the gait. I allow the horse to run around me once or twice and then bring him to a trot. After a few turns at the trot, and when he approaches the same position near the fence line, I again command him to canter.

Afterwards, I allow him to walk a while and settle down. Then I halt him, turn him around and repeat the process going counterclockwise. If I get a few immediate starts at the canter I am content for the day and allow the horse to walk off his excitement.

While the canter is easy to obtain, control of the gait requires skill. Once your horse has taken the canter he will probably lean on the lunge line and travel crookedly—his head turned inward while his quarters follow an outside track. Don't hold the lunge line in a steady pull. You must give and take, even though every time you give, your horse seems to want to take even more and drag you around the arena. *Patience.*

*Training on the lunge progresses from the firm
foundation established at the walk. Notice that at all
gaits the horse is moving on a light contact. Any pulling*

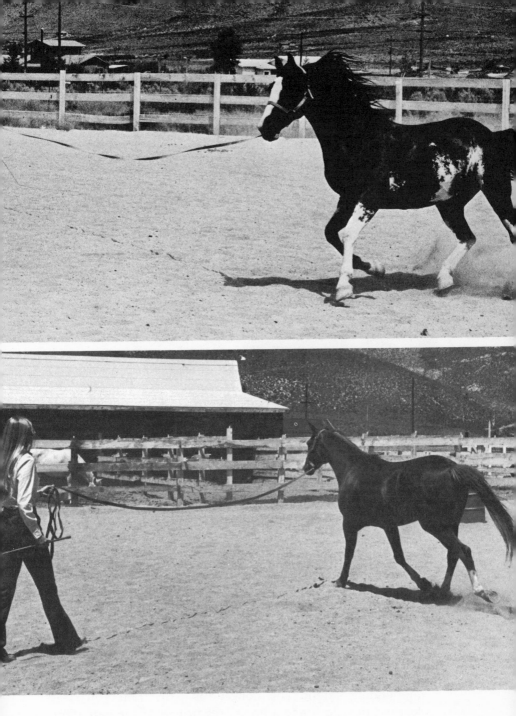

by the horse at the faster gaits is a good indication that
the horse has been rushed in his training.

Some horses at the canter for the first time on the lunge line are like a roaring fire. Try to instill calmness by some soothing remarks like, "Easy now, easy . . ." What you have to do essentially is wait until that fire in your horse simmers. I need hardly mention that your whip should be pointed to the ground. And do not attempt to slow the horse down. He will slow himself once he is over his initial excitement, which is helped by allowing him to canter on a large circle since he will find his balance faster than on a small radius. Your horse just may work up a sweat until he starts to settle. The moment he does, slow him to a walk. Allow him a good ten minutes' walk to think the matter over.

Happy to say, not all horses will respond with such strong emotions. Some behave quietly. But I do want to emphasize the most that can happen, since it is at the canter, I have noticed, that novices begin to doubt themselves because their horses proved a strain on their self-confidence. But anytime this work on the lunge line plagues you with self-doubts, just remember that running a horse around a circle is easy for anybody, but training control requires practice and patience.

From here on, time and repetition are your best training assistants. After your horse responds to the verbal command, go on to working him to canter from a walk; canter to a walk; trot to a canter; canter to a trot. As with the walk and trot, you can also work at extending and collecting the canter, although the collected canter on the lunge requires the slowest development or it will not work.

You will have noticed that I have allowed more time in detailing work at the walk than at the trot and canter. The reason is not slackness on my part. It is because if you have developed the horse's walk on a slight contact, and he can moderately extend and collect his gait, then you have learned how to lunge a horse, regardless of the gait. Your attainment will enable you to handle the faster paces—and in your own style. Therefore, the only further suggestion I can make is for you to realize your potentialities and your sense of *feel* while working your horse at the walk.

Sometime after your horse has learned lunge line work at the walk, teach him to reverse through the middle of the circle. As with much of lunging, teaching a change through the middle is not as difficult as the ability to interfere as little as possible with the idea you are trying to impart to the horse. Essentially, in response to your body position, your horse should leave the circle, pass smoothly through the middle, and return to the circle going in the reverse direction.

You are aware, by now, that any interruption in some already established procedure confuses the horse. In this instance, you are breaking into his pattern of moving along a circle. As far as he is concerned, you are changing the ground rules already taught him. When you attempt your first change of direction through the center, your horse will probably stop. He's wondering: *"What are you doing?"*

Consequently, if you can be agile enough to change your body position quickly and smoothly and get to his opposite side while urging him on, you might get him to reverse direction on the first attempt, without his halting. If you don't, you should not feel that you have failed. Merely work at the procedure until you convey the idea to the horse.

You start as you began in teaching him the first lessons at the walk—that is, with a long halter shank, a riding crop, and your horse walking around you to the left in a five- or six-foot circle. At this juncture, the halter shank should be held in your left hand and the riding crop in your right hand.

Now, while urging your horse with the verbal command, "alk," to keep him at a lively pace, pass your whip to your left hand, pointing it down. Just as smoothly, reach overhand with your right hand and grab the halter shank to arm's length. Next—and this is all one smooth transition—pass in front of your horse while pulling the halter shank to turn him toward the center, and finish your pass to the off-side of the horse. As you reach this off-side, let the end of the shank still in your left hand loose and allow your right hand to slide down the end of the shank. If the horse has not stopped in his turn toward the center you now have him passing to the center on a slack halter shank. While passing to the horse's off-side, keep repeating the verbal command. Lift your whip and, if necessary, touch him on the rump to keep him moving. As he takes up the slack and feels the end of the shank on the halter, he will start on the circle in the opposite direction. If your horse stops as you are making your pass across his front, continue your move and when you arrive on his off-side, urge him into a walk.

Perfect your style quickly to encourage him into a continuous movement for reversing. Otherwise, you may set up in his mind the habit of stopping when you pass in front of him.

You should see why this is so. In previous ground training, your body cue for the horse to stop was to step toward his front. Consequently, your horse is ready to react to this body position. For this reason it is important that you pull on the halter shank with the right hand firmly enough to start him toward the center while you quickly change your position from his front end to his off-side and toward his rear while urging him with voice and whip to continue walking. Remember, a horse cannot concentrate on two ideas at one time, so it is essential that you swiftly get by the cue that urges him to stop and into the position that urges him to keep moving at the walk, but in the opposite direction. But don't be so speedy that your sudden flurry of motion startles the horse and causes him to halt! To move quickly with smoothness is what you must develop.

Teaching a horse to change direction begins with a shorter halter shank, as explained in the text.

Actually, the procedure is not as difficult as it sounds, but the series of cues—body position, whip and pulling on the halter shank—do require a smooth meshing together to arrive at an equally smooth change of direction by the horse. To teach the horse to change from right to left, reverse the cues.

Once your horse has the idea, begin working the changes at greater distances. Little adjustment will be necessary on your part other than being certain you have control over the lunge line. Its slack tends to increase as you move across his path and he might step over it. The chance of this happening increases considerably when you change the horse's direction at the trot. If he is energetic and moving at a fair clip, you will have to increase your speed and the manipulation of the lunge line while passing in front of him. But by now your speed of movement shouldn't upset your horse, as he is now conditioned to your maneuvering.

There is one uncompromising word of caution: *Never hit your horse with the whip as he passes by you while making his reverse.* That center of ground is neutral territory. If you should strike him on the flank as he goes by, he will soon decide that is a "hot spot" to avoid. I am not saying you can't touch him lightly with the whip to encourage him on, but never, never strike him.

(One other, and often disregarded, consideration in lunging is the use of shin and ankle boots on the horse. I have seen people purchase elaborate and expensive lunging halters, which I feel is unnecessary, but hesitate to

The series of photographs on the following pages shows the horse responding to the handler's change of position. If one wished, he could cue the horse with the verbal command "switch." But I feel that the body cue suffices and does not burden the horse's mind with additional verbal cues, since "alk" and "trrott" and "canter!" are necessary and important.

purchase leg protectors for the horse. Granted, leg protectors are not absolutely essential, but for their price they provide worthwhile protection from the horse's knocking himself in lunging work. Some horses, particularly in extended work, have a tendency to hit themselves and raise ugly bruises which can lame them for a day or two. If your horse is the sort that seems to have four left hooves, definitely invest in shin and ankle boots.)

Aside from the benefits lunging provides you in learning training principles and horse behavior, it is important also for developing your horse's balance, suppleness and obedience. You can derive these advantages only from a proper lunging program. Too frequently, lunging is practiced as a quick-run-around in a circle without any idea of benefiting the horse's physical and mental capabilities. What is rarely done is to sustain the work at the gaits to the point where the horse settles down at the pace to develop balance, suppleness and mental conditioning.

Here's a comparison. A plane taking off is all speed and power as it climbs to its cruising altitude. When it reaches that point, the engine is throttled down, flaps are leveled and the plane flies smoothly and efficiently.

What usually happens in lunging is that the horse is lunged with speed and power and, just when it is starting to "cruise," is stopped. It is during the "cruising" phase when he starts to develop. By then he is settling down (I am speaking primarily of the trot and canter) and his gaits are becoming rhythmic and balanced in a steady cadence.

This is what you want to instill in your horse, along with calmness, so that eventually, when you ask for a canter from a walk, he automatically takes this cruising speed and does not rush about. If you stop him each time he is rushing, that is what he will always do—rush. But if you allow him to cruise, and fix the idea in his mind that he does not have to rush, this nice, smooth pace will prevail.

The same with the trot. This gait is probably the best

for suppling, yet you must allow the horse time to rid himself of excess energy and settle into a smooth and balanced pace. When your horse reaches this point, it is time to allow him to work, to condition his mind to the performance you want on the lunge line.

When I lunge my horses I allow them to trot at their own pace to allow themselves to loosen-up and get mentally set for the workout. After about a minute, they usually "change gears" and are ready to work. I keep them at that pace for about three minutes, bring them back to a walk for a minute, change directions with another minute walk, and then put them back into the trot. I use a lot of walking between gaits, but the horse does finish his lunging exercises with a conditioning workout. Muscles and lungs are exercised, and his sense of rhythm and pace kept smooth.

I would be considerably amiss if I did not mention the use of a surcingle and side-reins in lunging work. It is a common enough piece of harness, often used for the purpose of "setting a horse's head." I'd like to emphasise here, and it will be repeated at length in the chapter on developing the gaits, that there is nothing like leaving a horse's mouth alone to get a good head carriage, providing that the developing of the horse's natural balance is progressively improved.

Lunging, as has been outlined, assists the horse in a freegoing style, allowing the horse to hold its head and neck naturally and, in extended work, to lower and stretch the neck muscles. Suppleness is consequently encouraged, from the tip of the horse's nose, through his neck and back muscles, and into his quarters.

Attaching side-reins, particularly on a young horse which has not learned to stretch and extend, will promote a resistance which destroys suppleness. Forcing an artificially collected posture on the horse produces an incorrect head carriage resulting from the horse frequently caving in its neck in front of the withers, or hollowing out the back, and inducing the horse to get behind or above the bit. All of this defeats teaching the horse to engage its hindlegs which is the true source of proper balance and collection.

This does not mean total disapproval of side-reins, but only the usual use of them. As has been said, "muscles can only contract naturally and easily to the extent to which they can be stretched."

Thus, proper use of side-reins suggests that they should be adjusted loosely, rather than tightly, to allow the horse to stretch its neck and, through impulsion, encouraged to seek the bit. Later, when through good engagement of the hindquarters the horse's head and neck have raised naturally because of improved balance, then he can be assisted to a better and steady carriage by a gradual shortening of the side-reins.

Personally, I don't recommend the use of side-reins, as they tend to defeat the specific purpose of this book which is to teach you how to train; basic lunging work is a major stepping stone to mounted work. Still, side-reins can be useful, especially as one develops one's own style of training.

This, then, is the art of lunging. It is no small challenge, but neither is it an impossibility. Just remember what your aim is—a horse working lightly and obediently at the three gaits with minimum controls. Keep this aim in mind as you develop your style toward achieving it.

CHAPTER
7

BITS AND BITTING

One of the clever observations of Benjamin Franklin's *Poor Richard* is: "The Horse thinks one thing and he who saddles him another."

No shallow thought. It is one, in fact, which reflects the problem that has faced man ever since he decided to ride rather than eat the horse. Closing that gap between the mental processes of man and horse is the essence of horsemanship—the art of understanding, training and riding horses.

For my purposes here I prefer to reword *Poor Richard* to emphasize the idea that the horse thinks one thing and he who *bridles* him another.

I want to stress bridling because the subject is easily the one least understood by the novice. Indeed, professionals, including this writer, rarely arrive at long-term, definite conclusions about particular bits or bitting theories and practices.

Now this is not meant to discourage you, or to suggest that you face a hodge-podge of bit shapes, styles and cure-alls. Bitting can be mastered if certain preconceived notions are dismissed and an endeavor is made to understand the principles of bitting. Believe me, this effort is miniscule compared to the value received in both one's improvement as a horseman and the horse's own comfort.

Perhaps the first notion to be dismissed is this: If the horse doesn't respond as you wish, change the bit. Constant bit-switching in hopes of locating one bit that works like a magic wand in the horse's mouth is a substitute for horsemanship. The practice is not only futile, but a sure indication that a lack of rapport exists. Accomplished horsemen rarely give much thought to the bit in their horse's mouth, other than abiding by a few basic principles of bitting in conjunction with proper horsemanship.

Let's dwell on this idea a moment. The bridle, through a bit, is your direct line of communication with your horse. Of course, other aids such as weight, legs and voice are communication lines too, but the bit, because of what can be accomplished with it, is a most important aid. It signals to the horse your desire. *Signals!* It does not force! Force creates pain; pain creates fear. Fear blanks out the horse's concentration on his lessons.

(You can believe, incidentally, that your own skills are improving when you begin to rely more on other aids and less on the bit.)

Yet, too frequently, pulling and yanking on a horse's mouth, or the use of improper bits (even improper fitting of bit and bridle) brings on evasive and defensive action by the horse. In turn, a rider is often led to try all sorts of gimmick bits which the unfortunate horse must endure in its mouth. I'm not overstating when I say that more horsemanship has been lost between a rider's hands and the horse's mouth than in any other area of working with horses. I also echo many other instructors and lecturers at horse clinics who report that the bulk of questions asked have to do with the bits: "What is the best bit?" "My horse throws its head—do I need a special bit?" "My horse sticks its tongue out . . ." "My horse bores down on the bit . . ."

Always, in the curious way of human nature, these people speak of their horses having problems. Discretion causes me to nod my head gently, although I would prefer to tell them that it is they who have the problems, chief of which is ignorance or misunderstanding. I know this is true because I question them, and their answers on how a bit works reflect a poverty of workable knowledge. They do not understand the structure of a horse's mouth, the mechanical combination of curb strap with curb bit, and pressure points which different bits affect within a horse's mouth.

I can understand some of their confusion. Just examine a saddlery catalogue and you will see a tremendous variety of bits illustrated. All shapes. All sizes. And some accompanied by cure-all claims almost to the point of misstatement.

I recall one catalogue displaying its wares under the

bold print of an old adage: *There is a key to every horse's mouth.* Then page after page after page displayed an array of bits. If this is enough to cause a professional to scratch his head in confusion, I can imagine how it befuddles the novice.

Yes, there is a key to every horse's mouth. But not so much through the bit as in the sympathetic hands of the rider. Have no delusions here. Virtually any bit is harmless with proper use, but even the mildest bit can be a torture device with improper use.

A good horseman uses the simplest instruments, but uses them superlatively well. Or, to put it another way, a good horseman is constantly improving his horsemanship, but not at the expense of the horse through stronger bits or gadgets. Sooner or later the horse becomes the brunt of pain and force, and here horsemanship ends.

A wise horseman then asks, *Where does pain and force begin?* A good question, because unless the horse understands the force a bit can exert on its mouth, it has no idea how to respect that force in a manner you desire as a trained response. Now we're getting to the crux of it all.

Obviously, any hard jerking of a bit in a horse's mouth gives him pain and destroys rapport. Less understood is that an overly cautious use of the reins (as if one were using sewing thread which must not be broken) accomplishes nothing either, not even rapport, since you are not communicating with the horse.

For years I was dubious as to how to teach a student to *feel* the difference between effective pressure, which is necessary to train, and painful pressure, which destroys training. Finally, I arrived at an analogy which proved helpful in demonstrating to a student a tactile sense of pressure and pain.

Have you experienced the sensation when someone takes a firm hold behind your neck, just below the ears? If you have, you'll understand my point. If not, have a friend stand behind you and squeeze your neck. Those neck tendons are not unlike a horse's mouth in sensitivity. Instruct your friend to increase the squeezing and notice how the added pressure, which now becomes painful, causes you to twist and pull away.

Now, you try it on your friend. *Feel* how little squeezing is necessary to control your obliging pal. You can induce him to turn left or right merely by pushing your thumb or other fingers into the respective side of his neck. But squeeze even slightly more and that is too much. He will freeze or wiggle out of your hold. You should sense the intensity of the pressure that can turn a gentle squeeze into pain. Excessive pressure can be likened to pulling on the reins. Those hard hands make hard pullers out of horses, just as hard pressure on your friend's neck causes him to jerk away.

Pressure allows control, but pain forces immediate rebellion. Learn this lesson and you will be better able to teach your horse to respond to pressure. And remember, the bit is a force in the horse's mouth. Until the horse has tested that force—and he will—and learns that pain can be caused, only then will he be willing to accept the pressure which, hopefully, you will now *feel* how to use. Naturally, how well you meet this test will demonstrate the essence of your horsemanship.

I urge you to experiment with this neck game. It can convey to you a good year's experience about how bits work in a horse's mouth.

Now that you understand the subtleties of pressure and pain, let's examine the horse's mouth for the pressure points upon which a bit acts.

First, study the cross-section illustration of the horse's head (Figures 1a, 1b). Burn it into your mind so you know it as well as you know your horse's color. If possible, look into his mouth (put your index finger just within the side of his mouth along the bar area). Now, take a good look at his tongue. Note its size and how the horse can manipulate

Figure 1a.

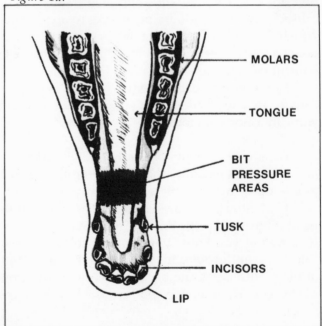

Figure 1b.

it. An improperly fitted bit causes similar reaction. Note the bars and the lay of the teeth.

The horse's mouth is not a complicated structure. All parts except the teeth are flesh, or, as with the bars, tender bone covered by a thin layer of flesh. Whereas the tongue is mobile and can offset some bit discomfort, other areas of contact with the bit are fixed to the head. Therefore, if the lips, bars, chin groove or poll feel pain, the horse can only react by head-throwing, boring, running away or just plain fretting—any one of which is detrimental to training or even riding for pleasure.

Different bits affect different pressure areas with varying intensity. Yet the conventional approach to describing bits tends to classify them by degrees of severity: the snaffle is less severe than a pelham; and a pelham and snaffle milder than a curb; or a thick snaffle is easier on the horse's mouth than one which is narrow; or curbs with longer shanks create more leverage than those with shorter shanks.

All this can be true in a general way. But it is an approach to bitting which misses the point, emphasizing for the novice the relative, potential pressure that a bit can exert in the horse's mouth. Alas, it also leads the novice to believe that if his horse is proving difficult to stop or control, then a stronger bit is automatically qualified. (Rarely is it believed that, perhaps, a *milder* bit is required.) Even more defeating, this attitude blurs the idea that a horse's mouth *must* be educated, regardless of which bit is used.

For example: to make a horse move forward we usually just touch its sides with our heels or the calves of our legs and the horse responds. Why? Because the horse was urged, somewhere in the beginning of its training, to move forward when it felt either a heel or leg aid or a riding crop. Once the horse moved, these urgings ceased. A habit was formed which told the horse that a touch of the heel meant to move forward or else it received a hard kick or a cut of a riding crop. Probably only a lesson or two was needed for the animal to respond casually to leg pressure.

But when it comes to stopping the horse, the rider uses a force on the bit well out of proportion to what is necessary to urge forward this same amount of weight!

Without proper bit education, too much reliance on an array of bits becomes an easy and shortsighted way out. With an uneducated mouth and uneducated hands, any bit can be severe, even those rated mild. Conversely, a horse educated in the mouth, and for hands which *feel* and understand how different bits act upon the horse's mouth, any bit is gentle, even those deemed cruel. It all depends on your hands and how well you have conditioned your horse to respond to the bit.

SNAFFLES

Bits are basically of three types, regardless of an inordinate number of varieties. There is the snaffle, the pelham—a combination of snaffle and curb—and the curb. The curb may be a single bit, as in a Western curb, or as part of a double bridle which includes a smaller snaffle.

Snaffles are further segregated as straight bar or jointed (Figures 2a, 2b). Both are direct action bits. No leverage is involved to act on the horse's mouth. When the reins are tightened the bit slips up against the corners of the horse's mouth and stretches the lips with a force equal to your pull. Only a little pressure is applied against the tongue.

The jointed snaffle has an additional action. When the reins are tightened the bit folds upward at the joint and more pressure is concentrated on the lips and also on the bars, especially if the hands are held low.

Consequently, and academically speaking, the straight bar is considered the milder snaffle. Mouthpieces on this snaffle may also curve outward in a mild arc. This is called the mullen and allows the tongue slightly more room to manipulate than a straight bar snaffle. The tongue can push up against the mullen with some relieving effect. Think about this as if you had a wad of paper on the back of your tongue—as a straight bar would rest in a horse's mouth—opposed to the wad nearer the tip of your tongue, comparable to the mullen. You can sense that your tongue will more easily manipulate the wad placed forward than farther back. While the comparison is a rough one, you can understand why the mullen is considered milder than a straight bar. Horses do go easier in that bit, particularly if the horse has to cope with a heavy-handed rider.

Snaffles are manufactured with rubber mouthpieces, which are soft, harder substances called vulcanite; and, of course, metal. Rubber-type mouthpieces work very well on horses that are nervous about their mouths and that have learned to pull to escape pain from heavy (jerking) hands. By removing the more painful metal bit, you give the horse less reason to tug. These rubbery bits are also fine in introducing the bit to a green horse or for retraining one which needs its confidence bolstered.

The jointed snaffle is the more popular snaffle. Some horsemen, particularly those whose lives are dedicated to fox hunting or ordinary riding, feel nothing more is really needed in a horse's mouth than a thick, jointed snaffle. I tend to agree. Not only does it mark a well-trained horse— if the horse goes obediently and confidently—but there are fewer reins to handle and less steel in the horse's mouth. The thick, jointed snaffle also allows the horse to carry itself more naturally. If one is entering show classes where a more collected head carriage is needed, then this snaffle is not sufficient. Still, it is a fine bit to return to now and then outside the show ring.

Jointed snaffles are linked together, cannon to cannon. Others have a ring or a spatula separating the two bits. This innovation lessens the nut-cracker action of the jointed snaffle while providing more comfort on the tongue and less chance of it being pinched.

Frankly, I have never had occasion to use these other types of jointed snaffles, although the claims for them sound reasonable. I have used many of the conventional jointed snaffles, and these have been more than adequate. So spare yourself some added bit expenses and don't go out and buy a particular bit simply because the claim is made that it might be somewhat more effective in some way than another. It is still all in the hands—and a thick, typically jointed snaffle is sufficient.

But if you should be purchasing a bit, or examining one to use on your horse, pay some attention to the cheek rings. Even the old-style large ring, which should be about 3–3½ inches to prevent the bit from being pulled through the side of the mouth, is adequate as long as there isn't considerable wear of the ring through the bit. Horses can pinch their lips with an excessively worn ring snaffle. Yet, some "play" of the ring through the bit is helpful in keeping the horse's mouth relaxed.

More popular cheek rings are the D-ring and the eggbutt. Their design prevents a bit from sliding through the mouth, and the smooth mesh of bit to cheek ring offsets any possibility of pinching the lips.

Again, slight variations are to be seen. Some of the cheek pieces allow the bit to "play," while others are rigidly fixed—bit and cheek piece forming one solid unit. One with a slight play between the bit and cheeks is more desirable if you are selecting your first bit. Someone offered the idea that such a bit has the same effect on the horse's mouth as chewing a piece of gum has on a human's mouth. Gum-chewing keeps the jaw relaxed and moist. A bit with play accomplishes the same thing for the horse, and is essential with a horse that has learned to outsmart rough hands, as horses are prone to do.

Just as important is for the snaffle to have a fairly thick mouthpiece as opposed to one that is narrow. Thickness is more comfortable because of greater bearing surface, and it won't irritate or cut the lip corners. Besides, a thick mouth-

Figure 2. Commonly used snaffle bits:

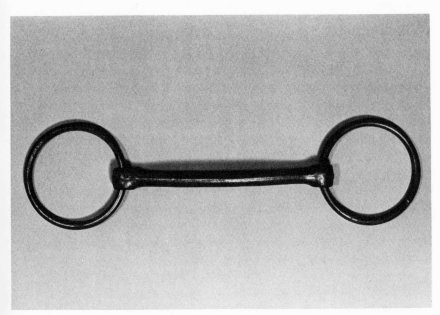

a. Straight bar with wire cheeks.

b. Jointed, eggbutt cheeks.

Figure 2. Commonly used snaffle bits:

c. Jointed, D-ring (or dee).

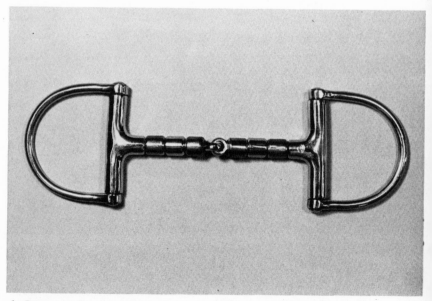

d. Copper roller mouthpiece.

112

Figure 2. Commonly used snaffle bits:

e. Copper wire mouthpiece.

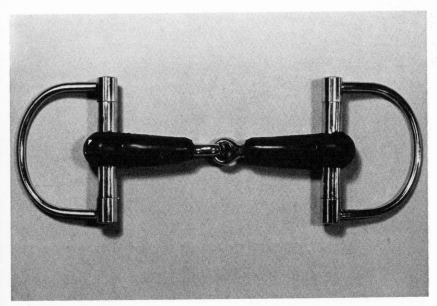

f. Rubber covering.

Figure 2. Commonly used snaffle bits:

g. *Fulmer snaffle. (The long cheeks assist in turning a horse and keeping its head straight. A favorite with dressage riders and used with a dropped noseband.)*

h. *Ball-cheek breaking bit with keys. (Preferred by some trainers for a young horse's introduction to a bit. The keys promote the tongue to play and relax the mouth.)*

Figure 2. Commonly used snaffle bits:

i. Bridoon snaffle. (Never to be used as a conventional snaffle. This snaffle joins a curb for the double bridle.)

j. Wire. (When all else fails—and that includes horsemanship!)

piece encourages the horse to move forward on the bit without fear.

As a novice, until your hands are educated to *feel,* a thick snaffle allows you and your horse a better chance for communication.

CURB BITS

Like snaffles, curb bits parade from catalogues and show-cases until the eye is weary from looking.

Compounding the confusion are a number of fierce bridle-warriors uttering lifelong experiences as to what is best in the horse's mouth. One horseman, favoring curbs, says, "I would unhesitatingly recommend a double bridle. This is the best bridle of all." Another, disdaining the curb, stands on this remark: "I have never used anything but a plain snaffle." Both horsemen speak from years of riding and training experience. Their statements reflect the opinions you will always meet in the horse world.

However, perhaps one more quote, from a bit maker, will start us on some clear thinking. He said, "Of every twenty bits I make nineteen are for men's heads and one for the horse's." Never was this more true than in the realm of curb bits. Unless design of a curb conforms to a few simple features which are adequate in conjunction with horsemanship, you will soon realize that many curbs are superfluous. A few, granted, are corrective bits with exceptional merits.

When one discusses curb bits in the United States, two types should be considered: the curb of the double bridle (sometimes called the English or Weymouth bridle) and the curb used on the Western trained horse.

Both types of curbs, unlike the snaffle bit which is a direct force bit, are leverage bits. You take less rein, but exert more pressure. This leverage also applies pressure on more than one area of the horse's mouth.

The curb has a mouthpiece attached to branches (or

cheeks) which are usually twice as long below the mouth-piece as above it. A curb chain, or strap, connects to the branches above the mouthpiece and rests in the horse's chin groove. The curb strap acts as a fulcrum.

Pulling the lower cheek branches (which are attached to the reins) toward you tightens the curb strap. And the bit, held somewhat immobile by the headstall, exerts a downward pressure on the bars and tongue. A slight pressure on the poll is also felt by the horse.

This explanation is simplified because a number of variables enter into the action of a curb bit: the length of branch above and below the bit, the type of mouthpiece, and the design of the curb strap and its relative tightness or looseness. All change the degree of pressure applied at the various points of contact.

Since the best way to understand a somewhat complicated unit is to break it into simplified parts, let's examine first the various mouthpieces and how they fit into a horse's mouth.

Figure 3 shows the lay of a bit in the mouth. The flesh, the lips and cheeks, are cut away to illustrate the part of the mouth engaging the curb bit, which is normally placed midway between the corners of the mouth and the incisors.

The bars of the mouth are the bare portions of the gums on the lower jaw. The tongue is represented by the dotted line. Figure 4 is another view shown as if you were looking directly into the mouth and only at the bars and tongue. The tongue, resting between the bars, forms a mild arc.

The bars and tongue are the delicate, sensitive surfaces which feel the bit. Technically, a bit which duplicates the shape of the horse's mouth and equalizes the pressure on the tongue and bar is ideal.

Figure 5a is a curb best suited to this principle. The tongue rests comfortably under the port (the raised portion), while the bit cannons extend and rest gently on the bars. This is a mild curb. Pressure from the reins signals

Figure 3.

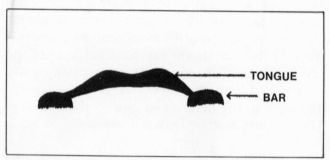

Figure 4.

Figure 5. Commonly used curb bits:

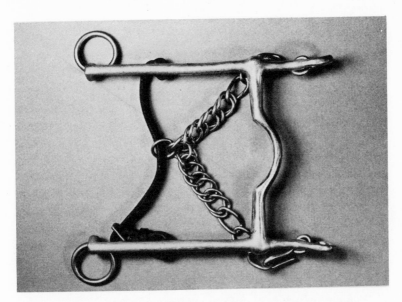

a. Fixed-cheek, mild port Weymouth. (Note the spread on the upper branches to conform to the widening of a horse's head.)

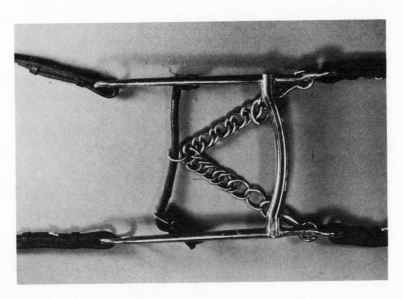

b. Arch-mouth. Weymouth.

Figure 5. Commonly used curb bits:

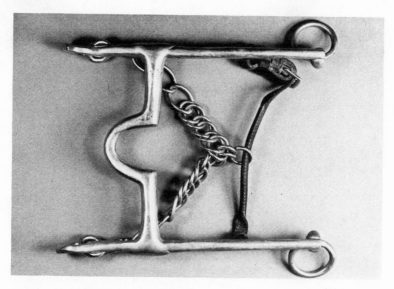

c. High port Weymouth. (Spread of upper branches not satisfactory, and lower edges of the port much too sharp to be comfortable.)

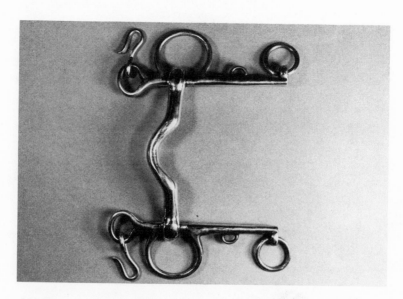

d. Mild port pelham, loose jaw (or slide-mouth).

Figure 5. Commonly used curb bits:

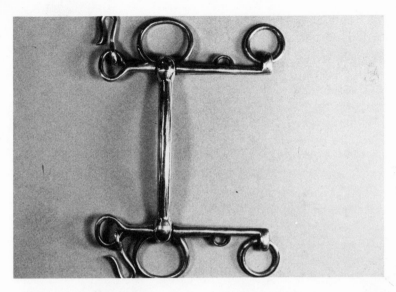

e. Mullen-mouth pelham.

f. Kimblewick. A member of the pelham family. Effects a lowering of the head when hands are lowered and reins slip toward bottom of cheek ring. Notice the square eye. Unlike the round eye, which allows the upper branch to turn in the cheek piece, the Kimblewick induces a direct and lowering pressure on the pull. Also considered a useful "change" bit.

the horse on both the tongue and the bars, and pressure is equalized across the width of the mouth. (Occasionally, you may see this style of bit with the cannons slanting lightly downward from the port, placing added pressure on the bars. Any bit so designed should be tossed into the trash barrel.)

Now, let's consider two extremes of this ideal curb bit. They are the arch bar curb and the curb with a fairly high port (Figures 5b, 5c).

The arch bar (and straight bar) curb mouthpiece is not, as sometimes assumed, a harsh bit. As you can now see, this type of mouthpiece would rest mostly on the tongue and exert only slight pressure on the bars. Visualize, too, how when the reins are loose, the tongue can easily lift the bit from any pressure on the bars. But when the reins are gently tightened, the tongue cannot lift the bit as easily and some pressure is brought onto the bars. Heavy hands, to carry our visualization a step further, would not allow the tongue ample maneuverability, and the horse, with no alternative, would open its jaw as if it were being pried (Figure 6). This is one reason this bit is not much used, particularly in the show ring where a gaping mouth is one way *not* to win points. Yet it demonstrates both how gentle and how severe a bit can be, depending on whether the horse is being signaled or forced to respond.

The curb bit with high port is, functionally, more severe because pressure is easily applied to the bars. This is so because the tongue, attempting to lift the bit off the bars is contracted into the high port.

Now these remarks about which bit applies which sort of pressure are not absolute. They are relative, for the most part, to how much force your hands are applying to the reins. If you were to apply an extra amount of pressure to the first curb bit we discussed (the low port), the effect would not be as harsh as it would be with the bit just spoken about (the high port). What's more, the horse would accept that added pressure with the first bit because

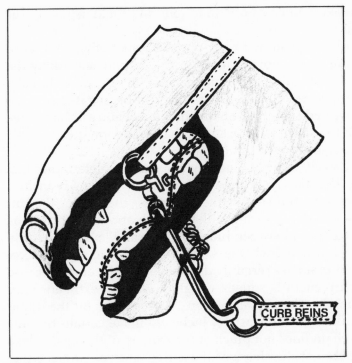

Figure 6.

its shape still allows some relief for him. But with the high port mouthpiece, that extra pressure would start grinding into the bars and certainly upset the animal. If you understand your bits, you know, too, that you could get the same mild effect with the high port as you do with the low port by adjusting your rein pressure. This emphasizes again that a good horseman is less concerned with bits than with *educated hands* which adjust to the different bits.

This high port is an effective bit. Sometimes horses, having worn a mild bit for a while, get slightly sluggish and a change of bit can work small wonders. The high port can make him take notice and remind him to listen to your hands.

Make certain with any port bit (especially a high port) that the port is not too narrow. A slim port will annoy the horse by making his tongue twist in the port. Equally important, the corners where the port begins its rise must be rounded smooth. The bit shown in Figure 5c has edges much too sharp which can cut the horse's tongue or, at the least, make him uncomfortable.

Usually, a novice looking at a curb bit determines that more leverage can be applied by curbs with long branches. Conversely, the shorter the branches, the milder the bit. There is nothing wrong with this evaluation. The bit that is well balanced between branch length and leverage usually has a lower branch the same width as the mouthpiece. Longer branches certainly do increase the leverage because the curb chain is squeezed tighter without extra effort by the hands. The key factor here, therefore, is for the upper branches to be at least 1¼ inches to make certain that the curb chain does not pinch at the corners of the lips. Take a close look at the shape of those lips and you will see that the lips flare out slightly at the corners. Raw spots are conclusive signs that the curb strap does not fit properly.

Now, this may be insultingly basic, but to make certain this matter about curb straps is understood, let's see how the curb bit rotates in the horse's mouth.

The reins attach to the rings at the bottom of the branches. The cheek piece of the bridle which holds the curb bit also has the curb chain hooks, one on each side of the bit. Pulling back on the reins does not actually pull back on the bit, but causes the upper part of the branches to move forward along with the curb chain hooks. This tightens the curb chain against the chin groove and brings the mouthpiece to bear on the inside of the mouth.

Notice on the English curb an eyelet midway on each lower branch. A thin piece of leather is attached to both eyelets after it is slipped through the middle, extra link of the curb chain. Called the lip strap, its purpose is to keep the curb chain from slipping too high out of the chin groove and pinching the edge of the jaw bone. It also serves to prevent the horse from the annoying habit of trying to lip the lower branches of the bit. And, finally, the lip strap prevents the loss of the curb chain.

What I wish to emphasize about the curb strap is that it is usually neglected in overall considerations in bitting the horse. Not infrequently, riders groping for some solution to their horse's mouth problem, switch from bit to bit, when all along the problem is due to the curb strap. It is *critical* in the proper bitting of the horse.

There are six types of curb straps as far as I know (Figure 7), but all perform the very same function. With English bridles, the single link or double link is made of chain. The single link bites harder than the double-meshed chain link. Leather curb straps are less severe than the chain and less likely to catch and yank those long chin hairs. (The single link chain is especially notorious for twisting chin hairs, so you should make a frequent practice of keeping the horse's chin closely clipped.)

Other curb straps combine leather and chain, with either leather at the ends and chain in the middle portion, or chain on the ends and leather in the middle. The latter may have a wide piece of leather which distributes pressure over a wider area of the chin groove. Some horses, usually those with short heads, may resent the wide curb strap, which could slip upward and irritate the ends of the jaw bones. One curb strap I particularly like is made from elastic. Because of its tendency to "give"—and this "giving" is so essential in all matters of the mouth—I wish it were used far more than it is.

Keep in mind that mouth problems of the horse should be investigated first at the curb straps before deciding to change bits. And if it is a matter of altering the force of the bit, you can change the amount of pressure by changing the curb strap. If, for example, you have a mild

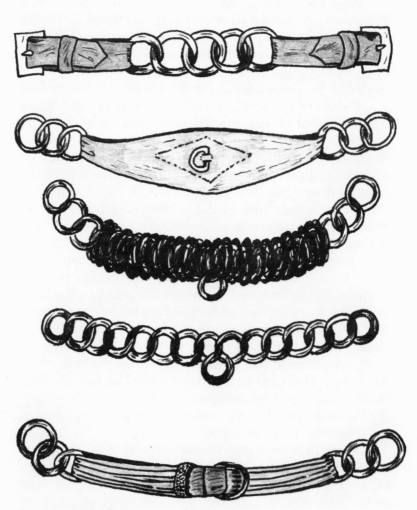

Figure 7. Curb straps.

curb with double linked chain to which the horse is not responding as you wish, try a single linked curb chain. Or a double linked if you are using leather. If the horse appears more than concerned about its mouth, and the bit is of mild design, then certainly experiment with an elastic curb strap.

As you can see, there are many things you can do rather than merely changing to a stronger bit; or worse, tightening the curb chain. I know this last practice is common and can make a horse take notice; however, with an extra tight curb chain one's hands lose the ability to work with subtle pressures.

The adjustment of the curb strap should allow the bit to rotate about 45 degrees before the curb strap tightens (Figure 8). This requires the curb strap to rest snugly in the chin groove and permit two finger tips to slip between the groove and the strap. Too tight adjustment and the slightest movement of the reins brings the curb chain to bear immediately. Too loose adjustment defeats the purpose of the curb bit and causes it to slide up into the mouth, requiring about a foot of rein to be reeled in before the bit begins to act on the mouth.

A 45-degree rotation allows the horse to anticipate pressure under its chin when the rein is tightened slightly and before the curb chain actually grips. *Believe me, this effect is not lost on the horse, which, if properly handled, will flex to avoid the firm tightening of the curb strap.*

The curb worn by the Western trained horse has a greater range of styles. From simple curb to ornate, silver inlaid bits, with a variety of port and branch designs, the Western curb bit is a study in itself.

Mouthpieces duplicate the general patterns of the English curb with a few exceptions. There is the unique rendition called the spade bit, often condemned, but actually a marvelous bit that allows a reining horse lightning fast movement. The spade is definitely not a bit for the novice rider or green horse and demands a delicacy in

Figure 8.

handling that is best learned from one who has had long experience with the spade.

Another innovation of the Western style curb is the mouthpiece with a copper cricket. This is a roller, melon-shaped and serrated, which rotates loosely on a small bar between the port. A cricket does not add severity to the bit. Horses tend to enjoy toying with it, which in turn promotes a moist and relaxed mouth. A cricket should be rather large, rotate easily and be *low in the mouthpiece.*

Western bit branches may be the so-called loose-jaw or fixed-jaw (some English curbs are also loose-jawed). Broadly speaking, the loose-jaw bit allows the mouthpiece, where it joins the branches, to slip slightly and contribute to the bit's mildness. More important, the better-made bits have the upper cheeks curve slightly outward to conform to the widening of the horse's face where the headstall loops into the bit, thus preventing rubbing when pressure is brought onto the bit. This spreading also holds the curb

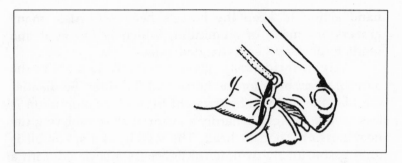

Figure 9.

strap away from the lip corners. Though I have empha-sized this aspect of the curb strap previously, it still bears repeating. Always, after fitting a new bit to your horse, stand at the side of its head and pull back on the reins until the curb tightens to be certain the strap is pivoting clear of the lip corners.

Some Western curbs have wider upper branches which incorporate a separate slot for the curb strap. This assures that the curb strap will clear the lip corners, although for most horses upper branches of about 1½ inches should prevent the curb strap from pinching. How-ever, be wary of any bit with short upper branches (or bits with only the headstall loop above the mouthpiece). These types will pinch, and the short upper branch bit does create a higher leverage than is necessary (Figure 9).

Styles of lower branches range from straight to layed back. A moderately layed back branch decreases leverage and prevents some horses from pursuing the annoying habit of trying to lip the branches. But the grazer bit (accessible and cheap to buy), with its extreme angled back branches, is the least effective bit for training a horse. It will suffice for casual riding, though, especially if you need to encourage a horse to keep its head high and extended. This head position allows the grazer bit to rest comfortably in the mouth. If the rider should insist on more collection, the bit tends to fall forward and even rock in the mouth, making it uncomfortable, and also requiring too much hand action to keep the horse's head set. Also, many grazers are made of aluminum, which is too light and tends to develop heavy-handed riders.

Weight, incidentally, gives a stability to a bit in the mouth; a *feel* both for the horse and the rider. So dismiss the idea that using a lightweight bit such as aluminum is less severe. Weight is hardly a factor at all considering the heaviness of a horse's head. The weight of a spade bit is one reason for the wonderful lightness associated with a properly trained spade bit horse. To carry that bit comfortably influences the horse, along with finely tuned hands, to tuck and allow the bit to rest gently in its mouth.

PELHAMS

The pelham bit, in that curious category of neither "fish nor fowl," is, nonetheless, much in evidence. Pelhams, as stated earlier, combine snaffle and curb action within one bit. As you might deduce, the pelham does not work as efficiently as the standard snaffle or curb, or the curb and bridoon of a double bridle.

Supposedly, if the snaffle reins of a pelham are tightened, the bit acts as a snaffle. Pressure on the curb reins causes the pelham to work as a curb. Actually, the curb reins tighten the curb strap with little movement of the mouthpiece. Therefore, longer branches on the pelham do increase the leverage, but through more pressure on the chin groove. This tends to fool people into believing that the pelham is a mild bit. Generally it is, but the chin groove can be easily abused.

Here's another problem with pelhams. If placed in the mouth next to the lip corners to act as a snaffle, the pelham is then too high to be effective as a curb. Readjusting the placement of the bit so the mouthpiece lies lower in the mouth to act as a curb, blunts the snaffle effect somewhat. To call upon the snaffle and counteract the curb's coming into play calls for some clever rein-handling from a novice.

And all from a bit frequently termed ideal for novices learning to acquire good hands, or for hands considered too heavy for the curb!

Perhaps it is this very contradiction which makes the pelham mild, since it does work adequately for many horses and riders. Perhaps, too, this is because the pelham is more suitable for short-mouthed horses which, to paraphrase, God must have loved for he made so many. Hot-blooded and better bred horses seem to have longer mouths. And while quite content in a double bridle, they would find a pelham less than comfortable. The pelham in a long-mouthed horse tends to ride too high in the mouth, allowing the curb strap to slip out of the chin groove and onto the edges of the jaw bone.

Often, when a horse is given a pelham, particularly a horse whose mouth has been injured or is frightened of bits from rough handling, a vulcanite or mullen mouthpiece is used. Like the grazer curb, it is not a first-rate training bit. But it does serve well as a "salving" interlude for an abused mouth, or for the rider and horse who get along fine with this somewhat self-contradicting bit.

One can go on and on about bits and bitting, yet little else can be offered until one's own experience becomes a factor in estimating the subtleties which enter into this intriguing area of horsemanship. You will learn that while it is true that snaffles are milder than curbs, or high ports potentially more severe than low ports, and so on, all are open to exceptions. And some of these exceptions are frequently learned (as even pros will admit, if you can weasel it out of them) by hit-and-miss methods.

You must try different bits to find one that your horse prefers and is comfortable in wearing. And just because your friend's horse goes well in a certain bit doesn't mean your horse will prance about with equal delight for that same bit. But once you do have a good *feel* of a bit your horse likes, do experiment with others to see and *feel* how your animal reacts. This will increase your knowledge.

Observe, also, other horses and riders. Watch closely horses' reactions with different bitting arrangements—the way they move, turn, carry their heads and stop. Notice their ears while working. See if they denote a look of contentment. If not, is it the bitting arrangement, or is it the rider's hands? Or maybe something else—a badly adjusted bridle, or saddle?

Many factors can sour your horse's behavior, performance ability or willingness. But most experienced horsemen agree that the root cause is most often found in the horse's mouth.

Incidentally, this "unhappy mouth" does not always stem from the bit itself. So, before deciding to change bits, perhaps you should check your horse's teeth. Wolf-teeth, located just under the gum where a bit lies, may be causing the horse the sort of pain you can feel if you press your fingernail into your lower gum. (Small wonder he's cranky!) Or, perhaps the problem is with the tushes (found mainly in male horses). They may be too long, irritating the tongue. This may be especially true on a short-mouthed horse with less room for the bit and will rattle against the tushes.

Tongue thickness varies too, and could possibly have an influence in bitting. A horse with a thicker tongue than usual and bitted with a thick Western curb mouthpiece (particularly a young horse whose teeth haven't grown to full length) may hold its mouth partly open because it is uncomfortable to close it. Teeth and tongue problems are not common, but do indicate the variables one always encounters in horsemanship.

Above all, it is the mild bit, properly fitting, which affords the horse the best comfort. With that comfort the communication lines are open between you and your horse. And from open communication you may proceed to that enlightened state where you think more of bitting as control going from the hand to the mouth, rather than from the bit to the hand.

CHAPTER
8

DEVELOPING
THE
GAITS

If you have watched horses loose in a pasture, riding ring or any place where they are allowed freedom, you have witnessed those wondrous sights which justify man's enduring passion for horses.

I have an image of a favorite stallion, an Arab-American Saddlebred cross whose one delight in life is to be let at liberty in an acre-size outdoor riding ring. Watching him enjoy these periodic reprieves from his box stall or daily workouts under saddle provides an exhilarating display of equine beauty. He is like a frieze from an ancient Greek temple come to life.

First, he gallops a lap or two around the arena, nose stretched, nostrils flared, sniffing the wind. (Horses, especially stallions, derive enormous pleasure from scents associated with their kind.) Then, after a few whistle-like exhalations of air, he switches to the trot; not just an ordinary trot, but that particular style only freely animated emotions give life to. With his neck arched and his body held in lofty elegance, he trots as if each stride were touched by a mild electrical shock.

Like their colors, horse's mannerisms and styles of moving also vary, each dependent on individual emotional springs. Some, like my favorite stallion, reflect the horse in highly stimulated poses of almost perfect coordination of balance and collection. Other horses, either less well-bred, aged, or simply not prone to easy stimulation, lack that emotional factor and manifest another form of balance. Most of their weight is on the forehand. And not only do they walk, trot and canter with less zest, but with their head and neck extended.

Make a habit of observing horses at liberty whenever you have the opportunity. Aside from the joy of watching, much is to be learned. By studying the way they move at their gaits, shift balance to stop or turn, or change gaits, you can see how each horse has a distinct ambulatory style. Even horses we consider awkward under saddle usually have a degree of smoothness and efficiency when free of a rider. In fact, much of what you will observe is what training attempts to duplicate—often to improve—from a simple turn at a walk right on up to the most advanced airs of the *haute ecole.*

Let's examine this idea closer to illustrate how a horse's natural balance at liberty not only markedly varies, but also prescribes different approaches to training.

At one end of the spectrum is the stallion approaching a mare, for example. Passion is the emotional keynote: every muscle of the stallion is alert. He'll nicker, raise his head and arch his neck and cautiously approach the mare. He is stimulated, both by excitement and caution. Thus, his gait is highly animated—impelled by active quarters, but restrained and channeling that energy and balance into a lighter forehand while his hoofs beat in even cadence as if he were tip-toeing. Compare this to the *passage* of advanced dressage.

The mare becomes frightened. She signals a warning to the stallion. Immediately, he doubles his caution. But the excitement continues to animate him. He slows his pace, perhaps halts his advance. But all the while his legs continue their nervous, impatient cadence—not unlike the piaffe, the trot in place.

Even the capriole and courbette, so familiar now from the exhibitions of the Spanish Riding School, are examples of horses reacting to high emotion. These, too, are refined under a balance perfected by a rider.

Let's return to my favorite stallion. There is a two-fold purpose in letting him at liberty. Besides the pleasure in watching him, he is also a good study for my students. For these occasions I usually have a mare close by. Invariably, the stallion displays the high degree of animation and balance just described.

Following this demonstration, I turn free a ten-year-old Morgan gelding. Whether at the trot or the gallop (which usually needs the stimulas of a few pebbles off his rump), he never displays the excitement or the brilliance of the stallion. Nor should it be expected. He is a horse, literally and figuratively, of another color. Not only is he less supple, but in his calm, even-tempered fashion he uses his gaits in an ordinary, practical way.

One purpose for this comparison is to demonstrate to the students the obvious impracticability of trying to duplicate the inherent animation of the hot-blooded horse on another not physically or temperamentally capable of achieving that luster. The attempt would be futile, if not outright cruel.

To force a head carriage from a horse that has not first been trained by progressive balance control, or to literally scare the animal into a frenzy to duplicate extreme animation, is the lowest level in handling horses. Yet, tragically, many placid horses are often manipulated into the imitation of the hot-blooded horse.

While my students, after observing both types of horses, readily grasped this futility, not infrequently their estimations of the training potentials of each type of horse brought forth some misconceptions. They almost always agreed that the stallion, with his suppleness and natural energy, would be more exciting to ride and easier to train. They were correct, and echoed a premise of Comte d'Aure, an eminent French horseman of the last century, who also spoke of the well-bred and exuberant horse as simplifying equitation.

However, as much as I could appreciate my students' appraisal of the stallion, and the belief that he was a *natural*, they were wrong in the idea that this sort of horse would be the best with which to learn training techniques.

A horse being a natural to train is far removed from his being *easy* to train! And aside from cautioning students against "over-horsing" themselves while learning to train, I warn them that horses which appear to be a simple challenge can be quickly ruined.

These spirited horses are already finely tuned. An easy persuasion in training is far more necessary for them than training *per se*. But when one is learning there is a tendency to constantly be doing *something* because it implies one is *training*. And just as poor training sours an animal, so can over-training cause a horse to rebel and refuse to cooperate.

Granted, it is a tremendous experience to work a horse with high energy at your command. *But make sure you can handle it*. Otherwise, don't dismiss the average, docile-looking horse. He may not have the brilliance you feel offers the best display of your talents, but he may be the horse which will afford you the best challenges and advantages for learning the fundamentals—and allow you some mistakes to boot!

I'm sure you could quote me dozens of examples, from horse shows to riding schools, of novice riders working at all three gaits on highly collected horses with a lot of zest. True enough. But remember, some highly bred horses are easily animated and collected through excitement. Often, very little training is required for these animals, other than the basic necessities for their particular showing specialty. True balance and versatility are often lacking.

The lure of brilliance must always be guarded against. It belongs to those horses who have it—and where it is developed judiciously through training. With this admonishment, I will go on to say what I feel should be said about dressage—the most enticing lure of all.

No other riding has attracted and influenced beginners to the world of horses as has the elegant displays at dressage shows and the *haute ecole* of the Spanish Riding School. This advanced equitation has done much to raise the level of conscientious riding in the United States. Yet, about two decades were required—since the end of the Second World War—for dressage to find its proper perspective in the United States and rid itself of arbitrary claims such as: *The dressage horse is the ultimate athlete. He can out-perform any horse which hasn't the brilliant patina of dressage in its training.*

What an erroneous assumption!

Advanced dressage has far more inherent dangers than benefits in the hands of novices who are too anxious to obtain the "dressage look" in their horses. Only a comparatively few horses and riders have the total qualifications to reach advanced levels of dressage.

More precisely, advanced dressage is an end in itself. Art for the sake of art, if you wish. Additionally, the advanced dressage horse (to counter another claim of the horse being charged with enormous initiative) is really a robotized performer. Its "initiative" is completely in the rider's hands to display the animal in a finely organized, perfectly controlled submission to a rider's equestrian skill and tact.

I am not disparaging dressage at this high level. If performed properly, it is a feat to be appreciated. But novices, starry-eyed over such performances, often consider dressage at this level as the sole expression of dressage. It isn't. Advanced dressage is the extension of *elementary dressage,* which you are capable of attaining. This becomes clear if you understand dressage as a principle rather than an appearance.

The French term dressage, basically, means training. Taking the definition further, dressage systemizes a series of exercises for developing and influencing a horse's balance for a rider's purposes, and for suppling and bringing about a handier, more obedient horse at his three gaits and the variations thereof.

There is a catch, though, which cannot be overstressed: *Dressage implies a quality in the performance or it ceases to be dressage.*

Dressage is, therefore, marked in all its progressions by standards—whether in riding a snaffle-bitted horse in a circle, or the *passage* in a double bridle. This standard is not based on scientific formulae where, once the horse is collected between the rider's hands and legs, the exercises are performed automatically. (This might be true to a minimum extent, but I advise you to dismiss it.)

However, there is a *something* which gives meaning to a standard more than cause-effect, and it is a rider's rapport and sense of *feel* with the horse. Rapport, to refresh your memory, is a relationship of mutual trust and understanding between you and your horse. Don't just read that statement. *Dwell upon it. Imprint it in your mind.*

This all-important rapport, or trust and understanding, must be conveyed by you to your horse, since it's not likely he will initiate the feeling. Rapport, and a sense of *feel* separate an enlightened horseman from one who merely sits on a horse. The former will get along with horses. The other type will give horses problems.

Obviously, your skill grows as you develop rapport and a sense of *feel*. And if all this is reflected in your horse's performance, you are essentially practicing dressage. So, don't be fooled by flashy outward manifestations of dressage. *It's the quality that must be measured.* This is worth a concrete example.

Picture a novice on an advanced dressage horse. Without too much instruction, probably he or she could bring the horse to a *piaffe.* But it would be only the outward appearance of the *piaffe.* More than likely, the movement would lack rhythm and impulsion, let alone the balance to keep the horse from falling behind the bit, or forward out of the *piaffe.*

In this instance, *feel* in a rider's legs is extremely important. Hands, too, would have to *feel.* Weight, as an aid, would also *feel.* All these combine to accomplish as perfect a *piaffe* as possible.

"Grandstand" riders often dazzle crowds with the outward facade of a *piaffe,* or other advanced school movements (circus riding often does). But a horseman who understands the true meaning of dressage would not be easily fooled. Nor should you.

What should matter—and I hope it will guide you in all your endeavors with horses—is *how well* you train your horse to perform. A simple trot, performed well, is just as important in an equitational sense as a well-performed *passage*. In fact, that trot in its progressive development could influence *how well* the *passage* is performed if the horse were trained to that level.

With this *how well* idea serving as a premise for your mounted work in developing the gaits, it is assumed you are a competent rider. You should be able to sit quietly and balanced in the saddle without bumping on the horse's back, use hand and leg aids independently (since unsteady hands and legs cause unconscious movements which interfere with training) and be able to ride horses with sufficient confidence to take a horse on to mounted training.

As in the dismounted lunging work, which is designed to give you practice in understanding how a horse is trained, these mounted lessons will follow the same idea. The following instructions do not presume to be an extensive training course for the horse for two reasons:

1. The less you ask of your horse when you are learning, the more likely you are to succeed, since you will minimize the horse's tendency toward rigidity and tenseness by not asking more than you can handle from one basic step to another.

2. On the other hand, you must challenge your abilities to perfect these basic steps, since to excel in any athletic endeavor demands a thorough grounding in fundamentals. Your thoroughness at the basic level encourages you to grow more capable and efficient by freeing the active or conscious part of your mind to concentrate on advanced problems or emergencies when quick thinking and action are necessary.

In the first section of this book you learned, from basic practice, how a horse reacts to punishment-persuasion techniques. How it submits or rebels to a command. How habits become ingrained responses, including the ability of the horse to learn verbal commands.

If you have absorbed these fundamentals and improved your abilities through work from the ground, then you have progressed more than you realize. You may have already attained a distinct *feel* for what you are doing, which will give dividends in mounted work.

If you have not learned these ground rules, then either you worked with such a sluggish nitwit of a horse (so get another) or, more likely, you pushed the horse and yourself too far.

Rushing training is self-defeating. Absolutely.

Many horses, particularly green ones, show a quickness in learning which might cause a trainer to overrate them (or himself) and push on faster with the training. But sooner or later, this will backfire. Patience not only means taking one's time in teaching lessons to the horse, but taking the time also for the horse to absorb what you have taught him.

Keeping this thought in mind will, I hope, slow you down in mounted training. Concentrate on the basic principles; perfect them, and you will then better understand that not even advanced training is complicated or dependent on an elaborate "abracadabra."

However, advanced mounted training does require a highly skilled rider, which is something else. The principles for advanced training, or for what is to be discussed here, are essentially the same: The gaits are developed to various degrees of control, stemming from control of the balance of the horse.

Let's break the concept down even more, since by outlining what is to be accomplished, you will be better able to evaluate your progress—and the horse's—and not get lost in hazy generalities.

By developing the gaits we're primarily seeking to improve the efficiency of the walk, trot and canter to your advantage as a rider. This calls for continuous subtle readjustments of a horse's balance; *subtle*, in order to avoid arousing its defensive nature.

As a point of departure, I will assume you have taken your horse through the dismounted work. And let's also assume he was green. He has now developed some agility from lunging and you have mounted and ridden him a few times in a mild, thick snaffle.

This is ideal for instructional purposes. Realistically, you might have a horse who has passed through a few owners and has learned evasive habits. You will encounter special problems which will require considerable patience on your part. Ground training would be very beneficial before attempting mounted work. It would establish better rapport between you and your horse which would carry over into learning to develop the gaits.

A most useful technique for helping a green horse readjust its balance with a rider is to exercise it through school figures, particularly the circle, half-circle, half-circles-in-reverse, counter-change-of-hands, the serpentine and the figure eight.

Additionally, the constant changes of direction assist the horse in learning to use its hindquarters from impulsion by a rider. This conditioning lightens the forehand by distributing the horse's weight toward the rear, creating better balance and smoothness. You, in turn, learn the use of aids which best help the horse perform the school exercises.

The one aid which you will use least is the reins. In fact, a good idea to assume is that you are not *training* the horse to a routine, but *conditioning* him. To train implies

Figure 10. School figures:

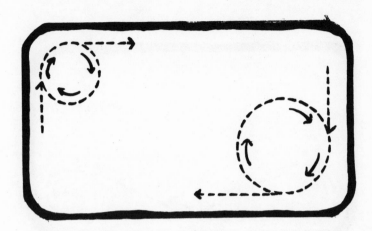

a. Circles.

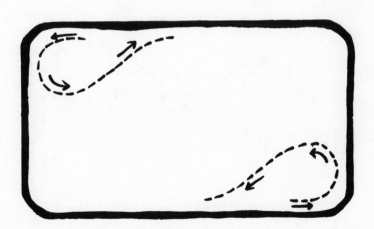

b. Half-circles.

Figure 10. School figures:

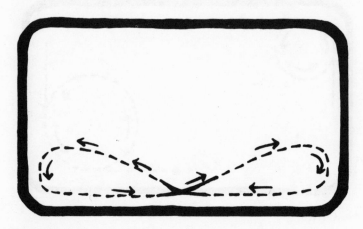

c. Half-circles-in-reverse.

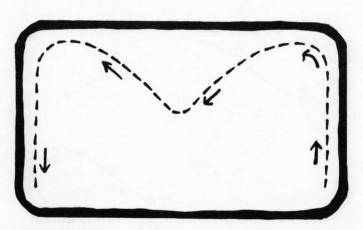

d. Counter change of hand.

Figure 10. School figures:

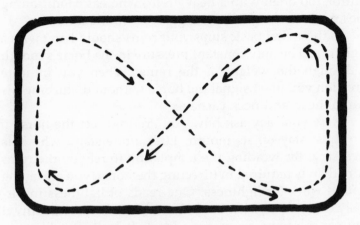

e. Diagonal change of hand.

f. Serpentine.

control, too often with a heavy rein, whereas conditioning does not—or should not—suggest as strong a hand.

In these first basic steps your reins should hang with a slight dip. The only constant pressure in the horse's mouth is through the weight of the reins. When you indicate direction you must signal the horse without disturbing his natural head and neck carriage.

Here you may ask how you are to direct the horse if you must stay off its mouth. First, understand why it is necessary. By avoiding the temptation to rely on the reins more than is required in directing the horse, you are laying ground work for lightness. One reads of lightness in virtually every equestrian book, but it is such a rare quality it sometimes seems an esoteric ideal. It isn't. But like any other aspect of horsemanship, lightness must be encouraged and cultivated by the rider.

The best way to direct the horse is with short, firm tugs. *Avoid prolonged pressure.* That could make him start tugging back against your hands and make for an unsatisfactory beginning relationship between his mouth and your hands.

From the onset of this conditioning allow the horse to learn that he has an option: *When he holds his head and neck naturally, your hands are passive and his mouth is comfortable.*

When making turns, signal with an easy tug of one rein. If this is insufficient, perhaps the horse will respond more readily with a double tug. Or, he might not care for any tugging (he shouldn't mind, though, as long as you're considerate). Anticipate, however, your horse's best response to the reins and begin refining those pressures. As an example, if he is distracted and turns his head to the right, put pressure on the left rein and hold it until he returns his head to its natural position. He will have rewarded himself, as the pressure will cease when he aligns. If you want to guide toward the left, put light pressure on the left rein and hold until the horse guides left. As he does, the pressure ceases again, teaching him that the response gave him an immediate reward. But should he require a tug of the rein, then tug. You must obtain a response in order to reach the horse.

Feel your way, just as you will in the use of your legs. But don't lose sight of your objectives: *The horse driving with his quarters, being guided through the turns with minimum bit pressure to encourage his natural head and neck carriage.*

Incidentally, few photos are used to illustrate the following training procedure because too many times novices try to copy what they see illustrated. Just as often, what they see in photos will not correspond to their own horse's posture, although their horse may, in essence, be performing just as well as the horse depicted in a photograph.

Each horse, remember, carries himself differently. There would be nothing more pathetic than expecting a nice head carriage (such as that of an Arabian) on a horse that is short-necked or perhaps has an upside-down neck. The poor creature just couldn't measure up. Besides, I want you to learn to *feel* your horse's particular balance (and his subsequent manner of carriage); to *feel* the effect on your hands; and *feel* the change in his way of moving. If you make this effort to *feel,* and steer away from comparing your horse to some photo or live model, I can assure you of greater self-reliance and further development of your body senses to what is correct for your particular horse.

True, it is frequently difficult to convey the *feel* you are searching for without a "live" instructor with you. Perhaps the following will serve to help you:

Sooner or later in your riding experiences, you will come upon a horse which moseys from the barn area with just enough enthusiasm to barely lift one hoof in front of the other. He has a definite case of the "slows." It may require an hour to ride just a mile. But turn him for home and he's all fired for speed.

This sort of horse, at his worst, could make a runaway. But most likely, he will gather himself, with his hind legs driving deep under him from a strong eagerness to get back to the barn. If it's an old routine with him, and he's had a tight rein to hold him back, he will tuck strongly and probably start that infuriating pseudo-gait called "jigging." He may begin throwing his head, since he has no mouth to speak of. He's highly collected—but all wrong. And if the reins are released, he's off and running like Man o' War.

Even with a decently trained horse, this sudden eagerness in the turn for home is not uncommon. But the better-trained animal will increase the drive of his quarters and lengthen his stride into a smart, rhythmic walk. There is a definite "together" *feel* about this horse. And with a light contact on his mouth the hands can follow and *feel* the particular oscillation of the neck, which is outstretched and straight. Since this disciplined horse is responsive on the mouth, he will hold this pace. But if you allowed your hand to move forward and lose mouth contact, he would likely try to renew the contact by increasing his pace. If that pace were then at its maximum effort, he would slip into a trot. On the other hand, should the rider decide to check him, the horse would shift his balance to the rear, lightening the forehand, and go into a form of collection.

The point of the comparison is to show that in the case of the trained horse the impulsion in going home would be *very easy to feel.* It would probably be more than could be encouraged in the school arena, since there the horse really sees no reason for it (other than something you are making him do).

If you have opportunities to ride a trained horse outside the schooling area, by all means do so. You can *experience* this *feel* of engaged hindquarters—impulsion— when the horse is offering it freely as he heads back home to the barn.

A green horse, after he has learned basic discipline, benefits enormously from outdoor work over varied terrain. It's also a nice outing from the routine of ring work.

Just as important, outside riding will give you a *feel* of how much your horse is capable of engaging his quarters on the trail home. Later, in the riding ring, you can better gauge the horse's performance: Is he really working or just giving a "so-so" effort?

THE WALK

Feeling a good walk is as basic to horsemanship as bar exercises are to a ballet dancer. Oddly enough, many riders may spend an entire lifetime with horses and still cannot explain how it feels from the saddle when a horse walks. Usually this is because their attention has never been drawn directly to the question.

Since suggestion is the first step toward perception, get on a quiet horse and start walking around the arena. Keep just a slight contact on the reins to detect the motion of the horse's head. Now, keeping the horse moving and concentrating on his front end (forget the quarters for the moment), watch his shoulders to detect which hoof is forward. Listen, too, for the sound of each hoof-fall.

When these indicators are sharp to your senses, begin feeling in your reins the swing of the horse's neck with the placing of the front hoofs. You should sense, and see, that as the horse's head swings left, the right leg is in the air, and when the head swings right, the left leg is in the air.

As for the hindquarters, concentrate on feeling, through the saddle, where each hind leg is at a stride. When the right hind leg leaves the ground, the horse shifts his weight to the left to hold his balance, causing the saddle to give a slight twist toward the left, and vice versa.

Now, to get a more intense *feel* of the entire motion, close your eyes as your horse walks. You will be surprised how quickly the *feel* of the walk transmits to your hands and seat. (Use this experiment to attain, also, a concept of what it is to ride quietly in the saddle.) You will catch the rhythm of the walk faster in an English saddle, which, by the way, is recommended for this early work in developing the gaits.

Riding school figures is a drill team exercise for you and your horse. As in any exercise, each figure must be done in a consistent, progressive manner to be beneficial. Figure eights must be accurate figure eights. Circles must be circles and not suggest half-deflated basketballs, and so on. Really, you must be careful in this matter. It is all too easy to ride faulty school figures. Some circles will "bulge" at one end or "fall in" at another and either of these faults will diminish the steady pace of the gaits you need to develop in your horse.

Unless you can mentally visualize these school figures while riding, it's helpful to place guide indicators for path outlines. Jumping standards or barrels can be arranged to form rough outlines of the school figure. Markers along the railing can indicate points of departure and return. Even a couple of lengthy ropes lashed together and laid on the ground can serve as guides. If lime is available, mark out the entire school figure and ride along the outer edges. Whatever method you use, be certain it permits you to concentrate on *feeling* the performance of your horse.

How large the school figures will be is for you to determine. On the circle and half-circles, less than twenty feet in diameter is too small for the horse to negotiate. He is neither sufficiently supple nor balanced enough to use his hindquarters for tight school figures. Moreover, you would be forced to rely on the reins to keep him in the turns. On the other hand, overly large circular figures diminish the conditioning benefits of the figures. Thirty feet in diameter is about the best size, and the half-circles-in-reverse is the ideal school figure with which to begin balancing exercises.

(Incidentally, until your horse has been conditioned to the habits you are about to teach him, don't suddenly slacken off after a few minutes work. Mark the session by a definite, concentrated period of exercise. When you are ready to let him rest, go to the center of the arena, then relax.)

With the half-circles-in-reverse designated, artificially or mentally, along one side of the arena, ride your horse from either direction along the railing. At the halfway point, turn into the half-circle, ride back to the rail toward the half-way point and depart on the other half-circle-in-reverse.

Remember, it is critical to properly guide the horse. Gentle indications, by opening or closing your fingers on the reins, are too refined and inadequate at this stage. Besides, you are riding on a long rein and do not want to disrupt the horse's natural carriage.

Your signals, therefore, are to be somewhere between a mild taking and withdrawal of your hands. This requires that you ride with loosely held arms. So work at *feeling* how much tug pressure is needed to keep the horse on his school figure route *without disturbing his head.*

The first few rides on the half-circles-in-reverse are mainly to adjust yourself and the horse to the school figure exercise. But you will notice and *feel* that in any turn of direction the horse loses his momentum; he leans into the turn with his shoulder and slows the pace. He doesn't drive with his quarters through the turns; it's easier for him to lean into them. Your job is to correct this lazy attitude.

If your horse doesn't display this lackadaisical manner of moving in the beginning, the diameter of the school figure is probably too large, so you must adjust the size of the figure. While you want large figures, they must also be small enough to cause him to lean into the turns. It is at this point that the mistake and the correction is most apparent to your *feel.* (Some leaning into any turn cannot be entirely avoided, and may be tolerated *as long as the turns are made by definite impulsion effort from the horse's hindquarters.*)

Now, start your school figure ride again. This time, when you feel your horse slacking as he goes into a turn, increase your leg aids to encourage him to drive from behind. If your degree of leg pressure is correct, you should feel a stronger effort. How much leg pressure? *Enough to feel the hindquarters engage without the horse scurrying into a rapid walk.*

Light heel taps, which obtain no response, only irritate the horse. Hard heel kicks may have the animal practically jumping out of his bridle, but you may have to get this rough if he refuses to heed your leg aids. Yet you should always think ahead and remember that you are conditioning your horse to take *light* aids. Start teaching him that the calf aid, if obeyed, prevents a tap of the heel.

That's *ideal.* And while it often works, especially with thin-skinned horses, others may require stronger urgings from the heels. Still, use pressures from the calves first. Always give your horse the option of an easier way.

Until your horse and you have come to terms about basic aids, you may have upsets in this early work. Don't let it rattle you. Just bear in mind—*one thing at a time.*

Ride the half-circles-in-reverse, concentrating on the horse's response to your leg aids at the turns. Don't worry, either, if you have to apply your legs dozens of times and through dozens of turn changes. You are teaching a habit. And habits which, to the horse, don't "make sense" require more patience.

After a few rides you should begin to understand why you must encourage your horse to keep his head and neck at their natural position while driving him through turns. Any deviation—particularly those instigated from your reins—and *the horse will lose the impulsion from the driving influence of your legs.*

It may take a dozen or so practice sessions at the school figure before your horse begins to readily respond. As he does, you, in turn, must respond with subtle appeals for *more* exactness because your horse will not let you succeed too easily. He will try evasions when you ask him to "work" in those turns. He may attempt to swing his hindquarters toward the outside. *Feel* when this happens. Correct with pressure from your outside leg, then *immediately* drive him forward with both your legs.

He may try to hurry his walk. Check him with a tug from the reins. If he pulls against your hands, correct instantly by checking him with one rein, right or left (hold the opposite rein fixed), and *immediately* drive him forward with your leg aids. This is imperative. The horse must *always go forward;* this breaks his resistance and causes the horse to straighten.

Throughout the lesson at the half-circles-in-reverse you are, step by step, correcting evasions which are bound to creep into your horse's performance. And bear in mind that, like humans, the horse's strongest urge is to *enjoy the pleasant and avoid the unpleasant.* When you correct him it must be unpleasant for him; not necessarily painful, but certainly uncomfortable. This way you are instilling in his mind the idea that if he moves as you desire, he will not experience discomfort. Your hands and legs are always "close enough" to check and urge when necessary—and *immediately.*

If you develop the *feel* for these exercises—and it isn't difficult—you will have learned an important principle of the art of training. So take your time. Remove any "clock schedules" from your mind about how long this training stage—or any other—should take you. Work at the *how well* premise. Keep the individual lessons short. Avoid excitement on the part of your horse and never overtire him.

The accomplishment of riding, properly and with ease, half-circles-in-reverse, and half-circles for variety, should give you and your horse a marked rapport. While you are confirming this accomplishment, you will become aware to which side your horse tends to work with less suppleness. Obviously, you should work the horse more in that direction, which needs more relaxing.

After your horse learns to respond to impulsion from your legs as he enters the turns, begin asking for the impulsion before he arrives at the turns. In other words, begin *conditioning* him to start assuming this energetic use of his legs whenever you ask for it. And when you arrive back at the mid-point between the half-circles-in-reverse, start altering the pattern and continue along the school arena, asking your horse to remain engaged on the straightaway. He will try to "let down" on you, so catch him quickly and continue until he walks with alert impulsion whenever you ask. And don't be fooled by a simply hurried walk. You want him to drive from behind, not just lean forward and walk faster from your leg urgings. If he tries this, check and urge. Get the idea across that you want impulsion, not speed.

Here, you may ask, "If I am to stay off the horse's mouth, how should I stop him?" Until your horse learns about impulsion, you can only stop him by gradually checking and bringing him to a halt. Don't attempt to make your horse halt on a dime. Allow three or four steps if necessary. If he was taught to *whoa* in ground training, you could use that aid in the beginning as long as you don't demand a rapid stop. Use the voice command gently, along with a slight checking motion on the rein. But allow the horse to stop easily.

Recall how in the bits chapter I said you shouldn't use your reins as if they were made of thread. Well, in teaching your horse to halt from the engaged walk with impulsion we make an exception. You should think of the reins as thread, which you must not break when halting.

This may not be too easy. Here's why: So far, you have stopped the horse without taking a strong hold on his mouth, or excessively disturbing the position of his head and neck (preferably with no displacement at all). He has halted by dropping down on his front end and leaning into the halt. Now you are asking him to stop from a walk that carries impulsion in its stride. And the halt must be accomplished without altering the natural carriage of his head and neck.

Get the idea? Do you begin to see how each phase of the training connects progressively? And why rushing or shortcutting creates, for the horse, greater gaps than he can understand?

So, once again, start your horse along the school railing. His quarters are engaged. He is calm. His head and neck are natural and straight. Walk through a turn. After a few strides take a firmer hold of the "thread" reins, and then, as smoothly as it takes to think *h-a-l-t*, stop your horse. If your leg pressure and the restraining pressure on his mouth was correct, you should get an immediate halt with legs engaged and head and neck held naturally.

It's a matter of *feel*. And if this is your first attempt to obtain a halt in this manner, you will not likely succeed the first time. It is not necessary in these first attempts that the horse stop accurately as described. It's just as satisfactory to have him halt slowly after three or four steps—*as long as he halts from the engaged walk.* So don't hesitate to check, release pressure, urge with the legs, then check again until you obtain a halt from an engaged walk. The moment you do, and it's not hard to *feel*, keep him halted in an alert position for a few seconds. Then urge him into an engaged walk to the center of the ring and again bring him to the engaged halt.

This form of halting is not easy. It does require tact, although not so much that you cannot gain it rather quickly.

There is also another reason it is not easy: You are now asking for a response from the horse that is opposed to what you have been teaching him, and this might upset him. You have, in the engaged halt, caused him to shift his weight to the rear for his halt, whereas in the past he merely dropped down in front. And your leg urgings have

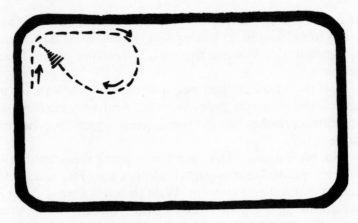

Figure 11. Half-circle into a corner.

indicated you meant for him to increase his hind leg engagement and move forward. Now, with that same leg urging, you are also applying a checking action on his mouth.

If you do have problems, and your confidence is slipping, try getting the halt by using a half-circle into a corner (Figure 11). Your timing is still important. Give your aids to halt as the horse is about two lengths away from the corner. This should assist in halting him just about the time he is thinking of it himself.

I don't care for this method because of the undesirable possibility of the horse's stopping deep into the corner and requiring head and neck displacement to get him out. Nonetheless, students usually are quick to catch the *feel* of the timing to obtain an engaged halt. If you decide to use it, try doing it without having to bend your horse excessively to get out of the corner.

Don't despair of your efforts to obtain an engaged halt. You might catch it at the first attempt. If you don't, stay calm (keep the horse calm) and try again. Be consistent, patient and gentle in your aids.

Your horse might try to pull at your hands when you

apply the aids. You know now how to handle that—check with the one-rein correction aid, and drive him on. If, after halting, the horse attempts to pull at your hands, brace them and let him cause the consequent unpleasantness in his mouth. As soon as he returns his head and neck to their natural position, you "give" on the reins.

Naturally, you should have your hands ready io brace (not pull!) the instant the horse tries to pull. It's the quickest and surest method of correcting him. Experience will teach you when to anticipate a horse's evasive ways.

Often, after a rider has obtained a half-dozen correct halts, he or she will fall into the habit of looking down to see if the horse is standing squarely. First, if the horse stopped with his legs properly engaged, he *has* stopped squarely. Second, looking down destroys your position and your opportunity to develop a sense of *feel* if your horse is on the proper stance.

If, through your seat, you sense the horse is not "right" under you, just a little extra effort to *feel* will tell you which hind leg is not properly placed. But if you still need to rely on your eyes, you could lower your glance (don't tilt your head or body forward) to see which hoof comes to rest last. Usually, it will be the opposite hind leg that is not in proper position.

Square stops, with your horse alert for a few seconds, are important. From this stance the horse can be urged from a halt into the engaged walk without leaning into the walk from his shoulders. If he does lean into a walk, check him slightly and urge him on with your legs. Then come back to a balanced halt and try again. By this time, you should readily *feel* the horse engaging his quarters to move into the walk. The gait may start having the *feel* of a lifting sensation underneath you, rather than the leaning sensation at the front end.

The walk has been called *the mother of the gaits*. Essentially, this is true. The conditioning of your horse to engage his quarters when walking, to stop with his legs engaged and to commence from the halt into the engaged walk is the quintessence of the future development of you and your horse.

Trotting, too, has its distinct benefits. Yet, if this is your first experience with training a horse, and if you are honest with yourself and believe you are only one step ahead of him, I would suggest you not trot at all until you have the walking work confirmed. Confusion derived by attempting the engaged trot too soon may impair your accomplishment of the engaged walk. Better to let him loose in the arena to satisfy his need to "let go," or work him out on the lunge line.

However, if you are a clever rider and can retain control, and are capable of coming back to a walk without disturbing the horse's natural carriage, a normal trot now and then is fine. Just don't set a pattern, like always taking the trot before a lesson, or worse, always after a lesson. Trotting before the lesson might stimulate him, but taking it afterward could instill a habit that says trotting means the end of a lesson. So, alternate trotting sessions, even using them for short breaks between lessons. But whatever you do, have your engaged walk confirmed before starting to school at the engaged trot.

THE TROT

The simple trot around the arena allows the horse the opportunity to relax in that gait and develop his rhythm. But give him (and you) a chance to find his natural rhythm, particularly if you are working a young horse. Many riders trot around an arena once or twice and then come back to a walk or halt. This procedure rarely allows the horse time to stabilize himself in that gait, to find a rhythm that is consistent. Naturally, I don't mean for you to exert your horse in these early sessions, but work him enough so that the movement does serve as an exercise in itself. Some horses need a trotting warm-up before they begin moving into a steady cadence. Others (hot-blooded horses) may need to be "cooled" before they are ready to bank their fire into a steady easy-moving trot.

Besides, how else will you know the *feel* of your horse's normal trot unless you allow him time to settle into it. This is quite important for you to judge at all your horse's gaits. What's more, if you have a lazy horse, you'll learn how much encouragement is necessary to get more work from him. His "norm" through laziness must not be accepted, otherwise he will be fooling you.

After trotting sessions along the railing, begin riding large school figures. You might start with a half-circle on one side of the arena, returning to the railing at the opposite arena side and performing half-circles-in-reverse; then back to the railing and into a serpentine with two or three large loops.

Keep your school figures large. Give the horse time to adjust to the pattern. After all, you are now working with more speed (not too much), and an easier springboard from which to excite him. Once you feel your horse has settled quietly into the routine, then, as with the walk, work from the half-circles-in-reverse and teach him to engage his hind legs in the turns.

While the principles are the same, in fact you are going at a faster pace (I don't mean speed, but your horse's normal trot after he has settled to a quiet pace); your horse's natural reaction when you ask for his hind leg engagement is to go faster. You must check him, immediately, and discourage this easier way for him. If your work at the walk was well taught, he will start to realize, after you have checked him once or twice, that when he feels your legs, you want him to engage and not simply go faster.

You might also have to enlarge your school figures slightly for the trot. Those performed at the walk may cause considerable bending in the turns at the trot. Just be certain the figures are small enough so he will try to slow and lean, giving you the opportunity to correct when you ask for engagement of his legs.

Again, avoid the temptation to proceed too fast. No matter how long it takes, practice this trotting work until it becomes second nature to the horse.

To summarize, you should now be able to walk and trot your horse through the school figures, and along the railing, with his hind legs engaged. From the walk, your horse can halt with legs under him, and recommence a walk from the halt with impulsion rather than by leaning into the gait. Through all these moves his head and neck remain in their normal position.

If you have accomplished this, and it's your first attempt at training a horse, you've done well. You have increased the important sense of *feel* and further increased your understanding of the use of aids. And if you go on to training other horses, or perhaps to teaching, you will realize now—or soon—that these first few basic lessons must never be rushed or shortcutted.

Now you are ready to begin teaching your horse to commence its trot from the walk with engaged hindquarters, and from the trot to the walk with engaged hindquarters, just as you did with the walk and halt combination.

From the engaged walk, you want the horse to smoothly gear into the trot without leaning onto his shoulders for the momentum to trot or increase the stride of its walk. Your leg aids, to review, are used with whatever pressure is necessary to obtain a response *and no more*. As your horse learns his response, you decrease leg pressure enough to serve only as a signal.

Thus, taking your horse from the engaged walk into the trot will require a firmer use of the legs and more tact in checking him if he wants to walk faster or lean onto the shoulder for his trot.

Every horse will be different, if only slightly, in responding. But I find that the following system works if you are quick enough with your aids.

As your horse walks on the long side of the arena, and

long before you reach a corner, increase the engagement of the hind legs more than usual. At that moment, the horse will probably attempt to walk faster. Check him instantly and apply your leg aids with more strength. Hopefully, you will have caught him as he increased his impulsion and, before he began to lose it, your stronger leg aid pushed him into the engaged trot. Possibly, he may have "leapt" into it. The form, momentarily, may have been *unequitational,* but you probably did get the trot from engaged hindquarters. If your aids were "just right," you may have gotten a fairly smooth transition into the trot.

Should you have trouble with this technique, do what sensible professionals do when they face such problems: find another way. Don't insist (especially with a young horse) *I will be obeyed.*

If you took your horse thoroughly through the ground training, you could use the sing-song verbal command, *trrott,* in conjunction with your leg aids. Another way is to begin teaching the engaged trot from a slower trot. I don't mean the "jog trot" of the Western Pleasure horse, but one slower than the horse's normal rate. (In fact, I recommend you aim toward developing this slow trot for reasons that you will see later.)

To this end, walk your horse through a half-circle-in-reverse. As he approaches the long side of the arena, urge him on with increased pressure. If he leans forward into the trot, accept it for the moment. The trot, itself, is what you want. The moment he breaks into the trot, don't allow him to speed up. Check and urge him, as necessary, through the turns of the half-circles-in-reverse. These constant turnings will assist in slowing him.

When the horse has accepted this slow trot, then work him out of the half-circles-in-reverse with engaged hindquarters, then practice stabilizing this slow trot.

Stabilizing is important. If you did have trouble obtaining the engaged trot at his normal pace, you possibly will have problems teaching the horse to drop from a normal trot to the walk—engaged. From the slow trot, you can come back to the walk with engaged hindquarters more easily. The slow trot thus becomes an interim step. Once you have taught the horse to go from the walk into the slow trot and come back to the walk—hindquarters engaged— you will have established the habit and can then transfer it to the normal trot.

Since the trot is an important schooling gait, you can understand why much careful practice at this gait, both in stabilizing and at the school figures, is mandatory. I can't overemphasize this, or the "corrective" aspects of the school figures.

Whenever your horse attempts to go faster or otherwise displays recalcitrant behavior, interrupt it by changing from a straightaway into a circle, or a half-circle, back to the railing for a few strides, then half-circles-in-reverse. However, don't switch directions so fast that the horse becomes upset. And by no means, when he becomes restive, should you suddenly let him walk to "quiet him." Do that a number of times and he will think: *Wow! All I have to do is act up and I'll be allowed to walk. What a break!*

We've discussed the possible problems of the trot. It might just as easily prove to develop smoothly. But whatever problems you do encounter, accept them. They are not insurmountable. Just as a calm sea never made a skillful sailor, neither does the lack of schooling problems make a good horse trainer.

THE CANTER

The canter, the most delightful of the gaits to ride, is the one the novice is most impatient to develop. The temptation to satisfy the notion, *Now I have my horse in all three gaits,* is so strong it is usually indulged. Not unlikely, premature work at the canter produces bad habits which are quickly adopted by the horse. And if old habits die hard with horses, those even recently learned from improper cantering are equally difficult to correct. You see, the horse prefers to canter too, but in his own convenient and often lazy way.

After you have acquired keener knowledge of the gait, you will understand why this is true. In the meantime, you can observe the most glaring faults of the canter at any horse show.

When I began judging at local shows I was jittery the first few times English and Western Pleasure classes filed into the arena. Horses and riders looked so expert as they passed by in the walk, jog or trot. *How can I eliminate without blundering and being unfair?* I asked myself. After the first call for the lope or canter, I breathed with relief. Riders were eliminating themselves. Some horses took the wrong lead. A few riders cork-screwed their horses to strike out on the correct lead. Some horses cantered sluggishly, while others galloped with high-flying front ends as their riders took a vise-like grip on the reins. The small number of reasonably competent riders who remained permitted finer judging analysis.

Rein-clutching is an unfortunate habit. It's almost instinctive with novice riders or trainers in the first stages at the canter. Self-confidence and a firm seat are necessary to keep one's grace despite anxiety when a green horse gallops off, or the stride starts to increase as one tries to stay off the mouth.

Starting a horse cantering too soon after green-breaking can lead to faults just described, especially with horses prone to hyper-excitement, and is axiomatic if your previous work at the walk and trot was slovenly. Instead of having three gaits accomplished (the goal of the hasty novice), you could end up with *three gaits in need of retraining*. So let me restate: Don't become bored and rush the schooling at the walk and trot, and especially in their transitions. Once these are competently executed, the canter with engaged hindquarters should develop easily.

Some horses, as you know, tend to be stocky or heavy in front. They prove the least capable of being trained to the light canter. You should realize there are moments in training when your efforts just aren't sufficiently rewarding. This may be one of those horses and one of those times. It's good sense to realize when a horse's conformation may not permit the best results you wish to achieve. But let's assume your horse is adequately suited to learn the light canter with proper training.

If you have taken your horse through the lunging work, he is already calm in the gait and responsive to taking the proper leads. This is a distinct advantage, although not necessary. In any case, your canter at this time will ignore such subtleties as diagonal or lateral aids.

With hardly any pressure on your reins, you want to guide the horse into the best advantage for him to take a proper lead. Not only that, but you want him to move with impulsion from the quarters. This requires an approach to cantering which will sharpen your tact. Your checking action against the horse's leaning heavily onto his forequarters must not unconsciously become harder. If the horse begins to go faster, check and release. Check a bit harder, if necessary, but not enough to lose your sense of control. This really shouldn't be necessary, since your horse, by now, is well acquainted with the meaning of a mild checking action of the reins. I mention the possibility of problems because when I've seen them occur, I've also seen the horse quickly recovered by riders who remained calm and confident.

The canter, to insure smooth departures and proper leads, requires a knowledge of leg sequence. If cantering clockwise, the stride begins with the left hind pushing forward and up, then the right hind and left fore moving forward at the same time, striking the ground almost simultaneously (but producing one beat) and holding support as the right front (leading leg) comes forward and strikes the ground.

For a horse on the left lead, the sequence is right hind, left hind and right fore, left fore (leading).

Going clockwise again, the learning cue for the canter should instantly precede the left hind in coming into contact with the ground so that the horse may strike off on his right (correct) lead. (When the horse is trained, applying the cue doesn't really require such finesse, except in more refined equitation such as advanced dressage. The horse will take the canter about a second after the cue when the proper leg is in position. However, if you have a horse that has the habit of taking an incorrect lead, then you should pay close attention to make sure that your cue coincides with the proper hind leg placement.)

Since your horse is being asked to canter from the trot (going clockwise), the cue should be given when the outside diagonal (right rear and left front) is striking the ground, and before the inside diagonal (left rear and right front) is moving forward. This way, you are engaging the left hind, which is necessary to insure the proper lead in the canter to the right. If you cannot feel the diagonals (and it takes practice), you need only to lower your glance to see when the left shoulder is moving forward or the hoof is striking the ground.

Of course, this is rather elementary. I would expect you know which diagonal you are posting on and time yourself to sit as you apply the cue to canter. But let's be certain. If you are posting on your left diagonal (going clockwise), it means you are in your stirrups (out of the saddle) as the right hind and left fore are in forward motion. You are in the saddle when the left hind and right front are in support and about to rise again on the right hind and left fore. You should apply your left leg cue for the canter as you *begin* to return to the saddle to engage the left hind.

This is all, theoretically, correct. But, if you have a horse that "trots-out," as the expression goes, timing is going to be somewhat hard to come by.

To sharpen your sense of *feel* in timing the cue for the canter from the trot, trot your horse around the arena, silently repeating *now* each time you are returning to the saddle. When ready for the canter, and approaching a turn on the railing, coincide *now* with a strong left leg cue as the horse drives through the turn.

The balanced amount of checking and urging to get a canter from a normal trot does require considerable tact, and you should test your ability in the procedure. If, however, you believe you are not quick enough, then, for the beginning cantering efforts at least, obtain it from the slow trot.

Begin by slow-trotting your horse to the right. As you approach the arena corner, check him slightly, alerting him (do not allow him to lose the activity of his quarters), and as his left fore comes forward to strike the ground, use your left heel further back than usual and apply a heel aid *firm enough for a canter response.*

When you feel that first cantering stride, *immediately* apply a slight check to make sure he doesn't lean into his forequarters as he goes into the second stride. Release and urge carefully with your legs.

A sluggish horse requires different attentions from your aids than one which has abundant energy to answer your demands. A lazy horse might he helped with the voice command as taught in dismounted training. Or perhaps a riding crop is necessary. If so, use it only as a supplement to your leg aids. The main objective is to *keep the horse's legs engaged* and avoid exciting him.

Instead of cantering, your horse may burst into a rapid trot. Ease him with your checks back into the slow trot until he is calm before making another attempt for the canter, and at a different corner of the arena.

"Suppose I can't?" you ask. "My horse just goes faster at the canter." First of all, stay calm. Start circling the horse through large circles (certainly no school figures like half-circles which would bring you out on an improper lead) until he slows enough to bring him back under control.

While this occurrence isn't common, neither is it rare. I make mention of the possibility so you'll be prepared. Theories are fine, but often experience involves coping with exceptions to the rules. Thus, if your horse *does* get out of control and you haven't anticipated it, I can think of nothing that would compound a bad situation more than sudden, forceful pulling on the reins to stop him. Don't get panicky. Use the circles to calm the horse.

Happily, the usual results of attempting the canter are less traumatic and often go so smoothly that you would be surprised.

After you have achieved a dozen strides at the canter, check the horse through his gait transitions to the walk, and then halt. Pet him. Tell him what a fine fellow he is.

Thereafter, repeat the canter from the same corner and in the same way to establish the response as a habit. The corners, as you know, increase the horse's chances for a correct depart, since it's more natural for him to lead off from a turn on the inside lead. But don't ride tight corners. The outside hind leg commences the canter and the horse mustn't feel he is being cramped next to the fence or wall. Otherwise, you will be encouraging an incorrect lead and will lose his engagement of the hind legs. If the wrong lead should be taken, get him out of the canter quickly and into the trot.

Some additional hints may prove beneficial.

Suppose your horse has a tendency to be lazy and prefers taking one lead—say the left. Begin his cantering work on the right lead. Work more on this lead than the other to offset his taking the lead requiring his least effort.

If he's spirited, start his cantering work with the lead he prefers. This type of horse should be kept relatively subdued. After a few workouts at the canter on his preferred lead, then work his other side. (You can learn which leads a horse prefers by observing him at daily liberty in the arena. You may learn that the horse generally takes either lead with ease—as nature intended. A horse that consistently prefers one lead over another is one that has become overly developed on one side and neglected on the other.)

Now, just as with the trot and the walk, allow your horse time to become confirmed at cantering. Once he is working calmly, quarters engaged, and taking his leads from either side, begin cantering in large circles. These will assist in stabilizing him and maintaining his impulsion. Later, and only when your horse picks up his leads correctly *every time* in the corners, start asking for them on the straightaway; first, from the slow trot, then from the engaged walk.

To recapitulate: With your horse now performing at the walk, his normal trot and a slower version, and the canter, don't mistake the extent of his attainment with progression. Rather, ask yourself *how well* is he performing?

Does he walk, trot and canter with his hindquarters engaged? Have you obtained this with careful use of your leg aids? Were you able to stay off the horse's mouth, using a free-swinging arm to check him, again with minimum effort? Through it all, have you conditioned the horse to definitely pay attention to you? Without fear?

If you can answer yes, you have accomplished a noteworthy milestone in your education as a trainer. If, however, you admit to some failures along the way, that, too, is noteworthy. At least you have questioned yourself and probably pinpointed those areas where you need most practice. A problem recognized is a problem half-solved. Besides, no one ever learned to train well without making mistakes.

An important step in your continuing education in horse training is teaching the horse to accept contact from your hands to the bit, putting more pressure on his mouth.

Previously, your reins were held loose enough to avoid much contact with his mouth. You were taught to use the merest "giving and taking" in turns, and a checking action when the horse needed to be slowed or restrained from leaning on his front end. Those light actions brought about the minimum interference (preferably none) with the natural carriage of the horse's neck and head.

Now you will learn how to move the horse through his gaits on contact with the bit. This doesn't mean flexing the mouth or the poll, or collection to any degree. All these will eventually follow from contact with the bit, but as a gradual process. Sympathetic support from your hands is required to teach the horse to go on contact. He is not to retreat from this contact or lean on your hands.

The trot, which has the least oscillation of head and neck, is the best gait with which to begin riding with contact. Following a routine exercise period, start your horse moving at his slow trot. Carefully take up the slack in the reins until your hands feel the bit in the mouth. After a few strides, urge him on to his normal trot. He will lean slightly forward to increase the pace. Without losing contact, allow your arms to follow that slight advance. If he begins to hesitate, urge him again, keeping contact and preparing to follow any slight change of his neck position.

A horse in his first training should offer no resistance to riding on this contact, since he doesn't have unfortunate memories about bits. So merely keep him moving energetically while maintaining contact.

For a horse that has experienced rough handling at the mouth, however, or is being retrained, taking contact can trigger defensive habits. With this type you will have to get clever, because he will get clever with you.

His old fears may cause him to suddenly flex and tuck his head to avoid contact with the bit. Keep urging with your legs and start him into circles, half-circles or half-circles-in-reverse, whichever is most convenient at the moment the horse avoids contact. Turns with impulsion, you recall, cause the horse to *drive* through the changes of direction. But hold a mild contact when the horse over-flexes until he returns his head to a normal carriage, which your contact must sympathetically follow.

This isn't as simple as it sounds. You have to be alert. Work at the school figure over and over until the horse gains confidence that you are not about to whip at its mouth. Gradually work out of the figures onto the straightaway. If your horse again starts to bow away from the bit, immediately return to the school figures. A great deal of patience is required when working with a bit-shy horse. The only cure is quick, gentle hands which never once betray the trust you are establishing.

On the other hand, if your horse leans decidedly on the bit and your leg urgings do not cause him to lift his head and neck to its natural position, it means that he has little respect for the bit. You have reached a point where bit pressure must now create a momentary pain (as discussed in the chapter on bits). Fix your right hand rigidly and jerk the left rein in a short, lifting action. Your fixed hand prevents the horse from bending his neck to lessen the effect of the correcting hand. This lifting action will raise his head and neck. *Immediately drive him forward to prevent his stopping or attempting to again drop his nose and lean on the bit.* The moment the horse's head and neck are in a natural position, resume the light contact. Let him think,

Going on light contact at walk, and (overleaf) normal trot and increased stride. In all examples, rein contact is light and the horse's head and neck remain unhampered: Perhaps you can detect, after comparing the horse's stride at the three gaits, a flaw at the walk.

For this particular horse, the engagement of its hindquarters is a shade less than what it should be working with at this stage of training. It has the look of heaviness in front because the rider has not urged the horse sufficiently.

"Well, on second thought, this does seem to be more comfortable."

Another evasion is the horse's lifting his nose upward. In this situation be careful of your appraisal. If the head and neck remain natural, the evasion is minor and you shouldn't make an issue of it; he will settle. But if there is a decided lift of his nose (you should *feel* the gait "fall apart" from the more elastic *feel* of the swing from active hind legs), hold your contact and urge him forward. This will convince the horse that he will receive nothing but discomfort for nose-lifting. The moment his head and neck return to normal, the contact should be relaxed.

Some horses will present habits which require these corrective measures. Tackle them by informing the horse that when his head or neck deviates, pressures become severe. Let him know that relief comes after he returns and holds his head and neck to their natural carriage.

Once you have the trot established on light contact in and out of school figures, then ride on contact at the walk and canter. And be sure you allow the contact to follow the natural balancing swing of the head and neck. You will then have established a firm sense of discipline with the horse—one which he trusts. And your horse will have accepted the bit.

However, just because he has accepted the bit, don't rush on to collect the horse. Many novices do. They seem to feel, at this juncture, that the next achievement should naturally be that finished look of the collected, balanced horse. This eagerness probably stems from a buoyant sense of accomplishment.

Giving in to the urge, however, would be a mistake.

Trotting on contact in approaching a turn. The horse is trotting with increased stride. Rider has lightly checked with her left hand and given with her right. The horse has the "mere" look of heading toward a turn with no disturbance of head and neck position.

True, the "finished look" could be obtained by an experienced trainer, accomplishing flexions and collection as one integrated step. It's even possible you could do it. But you would be omitting vital, separate steps that will be needed to improve your sense of *feel.*

If you did start collecting your horse at this time, and your uncertainties of *feel* in a situation caused him to become restive, you might cause him to get behind the bit. Should you fail to sense through your hands, or through your seat, when your horse loses his engagement, you would blissfully ride along with the *pose* of a collected horse—until you realized you weren't getting responses from him without taking up much more rein than necessary.

So, before trying to collect the horse, be sure he is willing to go out onto the hand without fear of the bit. For while he has accepted the bit, *you still want him to go onto the bit by accepting more support.*

This indicates increasing the stride. (I avoid using the implied term *extended gaits* because it is associated with particular performance standards which confuse the novice. Extended gaits are best observed at dressage shows, where you can actually see their action, something the written word cannot describe.) If, by increasing the stride, your horse works at the standards of the regulation strong trot, that is fine. More importantly, it is up to you to *feel*

Riding at the stabilized trot with no contact. Almost! What really happened is an unrehearsed example of aids correcting a slight deviation by the horse. The horse's attention wandered to the photographer (note excessive looseness of left rein). Rider fixed her right hand (note taut right rein) which brought pressure to bear as horse turned its head. At this instant when the camera shutter clicked, the horse is starting to correct its head carriage as the rider starts urging with her legs.

that the stride is increased while keeping your senses tuned to the tempo and rhythm of the stride.

Tempo is the beat of the gait. Rhythm suggests the regular recurrence of the beat. The tempo must not become hurried. If you allow the horse to go too fast, his balance, at this point, will be lost and he will automatically pop his legs out in front to save it. This is not increasing the stride, but hurrying it.

An increase of the stride does increase the tempo of the gait, but by developing the impulsion of the hind-quarters. In turn, the shoulder action of the horse is increased too, and his center of gravity will remain further back because the hind legs are assuming more support.

Because of conformation inadequacies, some horses never acquire true extended work, especially at the trot. But any horse should be able to go with more support on the bit and increase his stride sufficiently for you to feel the difference between building the tempo (with a rhythm) and hurrying.

Again, that blessed training gait, the trot, is the one with which to commence increasing the stride. With your horse at the normal trot, go around the arena a few times to make sure he is warming and moving at a steady tempo. As you begin leaving a corner of the short end of the arena onto the long straightaway, increase the pressure from your legs. The tempo should increase, but your hands, softly fixed, do not permit the horse to go much faster. Hands and legs must coordinate to leave your horse no alternative but to increase his stride. You should immediately detect more power at work from the hindquarters. And since the horse is not permitted to lean forward, he accepts more support from your hands.

As with all training procedures, increasing the stride should not be rushed; develop it gradually by making liberal use of the counter change of hand and diagonal change of hand. At all corners, slow your horse to his normal trot. Turning at the increased stride could be strenuous and unhandy for the horse to negotiate. And with the work at the school figures, the turns must be large enough not to pinch and disrupt the gaits, but small enough to cause the horse to work.

It may be that your horse already takes his walk with vigorous strides. If so, don't push him to the extent that his movement begins to resemble the human wiggle in Olympic walking marathons. Ask for only slightly more than his normal stride.

The spirited horse will undoubtedly understand your demands and be more than willing to obey. It is you who must use caution. Should you force too much, he will shorten and hurry his steps to keep his balance. And since this exercise is meant to allow *just enough* extension of the head and neck to permit the horse to go on the bit with an increased stride, your hands must follow the natural nod of his head in the gait, maintaining that soft flexibility on his mouth that aids in increasing a gait's stride.

If your horse is a dullard, use your leg aids alternately to encourage each hind leg to take a longer step. If you're still uncertain of your sense of *feel* (you shouldn't be), use your right leg as the right fore leg of the horse swings back (you can see the shoulder moving back). This is the moment when the right hind leg is ready to make contact with the ground.

Increasing the stride of the canter is more difficult. The gait itself is one of certain imperfections (a tendency toward crookedness, for example). It should be developed more slowly to prevent the horse's forming any stiffness and defensive habits. (Actually, this is true in all the gaits, but at the canter the idea should be doubly stressed.) Excitement and loss of balance not only diminish the pleasure of riding this most joyful gait, but set up resistances which hollow the spine, prevent proper head carriage and disengage the hind legs.

Having taken the canter (preferably from the side where the horse is more supple, to minimize arousing excitement), allow him a turn or two around the arena. Then, as with the other gaits, encourage him to increase his stride while your hands maintain contact at his mouth in harmony with the movements of his head. You should definitely *feel* a stronger support by the horse at your hands. Adjust your leg aids to maintain that feel.

After a dozen or so strides, return him to his normal canter by closing your fingers to bring a mild pressure on his mouth. Keep your hands light and giving as the horse responds. By now you should realize that your transitions in lengthening the stride and returning to the normal pace are not accomplished within a stride or two after giving your aid indications to the horse. This will occur later. But at the start, always allow whatever time is necessary—ten strides, twenty strides—for the horse to readjust through transitions as calmly as possible.

As you guide your horse into smooth transitions, *feel* the balance between your hands and legs. But beware of allowing the horse to straighten himself out into a full gallop. That is not an increase in the stride but, technically, another gait.

Provided that throughout these training lessons you have not abused the horse's mouth nor disrupted his natural head carriage; and, if you have concentrated on teaching him to respond to your leg aids with impulsion at correct school figures and on the straightaway; and have used your hands to direct and control the horse mildly, you will have noticed and will have *felt* improved suppleness, calmness and balance.

Once the horse moves readily onto the bit, control and carriage refinement are improved through teaching flexion of the mouth and then the poll. One follows the other, both leading into a measure of direct flexion.

This work will indicate *how well* you have done thus far. If the horse responds by "giving" and you can *feel* him "bundle up," or gathering himself between your hands and legs (it won't be much, but it should be there), then you have succeeded very well.

(If, instead, the horse lifts his neck rather high and tucks excessively; if the hind legs *feel* as though they are working behind the horse and not distinctly underneath you, you still have resistance. The horse has not elected to go on the bit. Nor is it likely he has been performing in his gaits well. Even more pointedly, this resistance boldly reveals serious flaws in the early training. There's no need to understate these evidences of careless training. Your horse won't. By his behavior, he will be absolutely frank.)

So, to begin teaching jaw-yielding, stand your horse, balanced and alert, and evenly adjust your hands on the reins with a gentle contact. Now close your fingers, creating slightly more pressure. Perhaps more coaxing will be necessary—say a slight trebling motion. Whatever, he has to experience a fixed pressure from your hands to realize he can relieve the pressure by yielding his jaw. It is a relaxed sensation which you will feel the instant the reins go light. Immediately open your fingers. As the horse's mouth returns from yielding, the contact is again established as it was before you applied pressure.

At the time of relaxing, your horse may open his mouth slightly. If he does not, it doesn't necessarily mean he hasn't yielded. It just means his relaxing response may have been light. It's up to you to *feel*, without looking down, that momentary loss of pressure. When it comes, reward the horse, as stated earlier, by opening your fingers to their position before you applied the pressure.

I can't imagine you lacking such finesse at this time that you exert too much pressure and cause the horse to poke up its nose. But if you should, and the horse does protest, check him, move forward to re-establish his balance and try again. If he should try to back, push him forward immediately and ask for the alert halt. Apply slight pressure as you ask him to yield his jaw.

Practice this jaw-yielding a few times after each daily lesson. It won't be long before you will notice your horse flexing the moment your hands assume slightly more pressure on the reins.

Once the horse is responsive, it is more important to transfer the request while at the three gaits. Start with the trot. As your horse moves with calm impulsion and your reins are in even contact with the bit, close your fingers as you did at the halt. The response from the horse should be immediate.

If the horse seems to slow his pace, correct with your legs and put him back on the bit. This time, anticipate and apply more pressure with your legs when your fingers close on the reins.

The tempo of the gait must stay the same. If it changes because of loss of impulsion, then the yielding was not true and you must better gauge your leg pressure to keep the quarters engaged and the tempo even when obtaining the jaw-yield.

The horse may bend slightly at the poll. When you open your fingers in response to jaw-yielding, his head should return to its previous position. If it doesn't, urge him on with your legs until he goes on the bit. Should this meet resistance, use your one-rein checking action. And *drive* him forward. Don't permit him to slyly adopt any "behind the bit" ideas.

After establishing this jaw-yielding at the trot, proceed to the walk and then the canter. The principles are the same. Novices, however, tend to go astray by asking for more flexion than is necessary. The results frequently give a "collected look" and produce much false satisfaction for the rider. It's just another example of the foolish "itch" to get the horse into collection too fast and hurry on to training in specialized areas. Jaw-yielding, poll flexing and light collecting should flow in careful progression as in all

In the joy of horses, it is more in the well-trained, obedient mount than in eye-catching beauty. Both young ladies trained their horses into enjoyable companions and themselves into talented horsemen.

other work thus far; and it's most jeopardizing if that requirement is not met.

Just as the beginning high-wire walker who tosses his balance pole away a few steps from the end of his walk is taking a chance, so is the rider who rushes flexions. He is risking the loss of his balance pole—the head and neck of the horse. A properly set head and neck determines the position of the horse's center of gravity, and makes for correct collecting and extending of the gaits in advanced work.

Collection, therefore, is never to be forced from a horse. He must volunteer the response from your leg and hand aids. This is the only way you can be sure the horse will stretch away from collection when you ask him to, or come back to your hand when you want that response.

With this principle in mind, you can progress from jaw-yielding to poll flexion. Trot your horse along the railing. Ask him to yield his jaw to your increased pressure. When he does, don't give as you always have, but close your fingers *slightly* more to take up the minute slack left by the horse's yielding. To yield further to the pressure, the horse flexes at the poll, causing the nose to drop slightly. I say *slightly* because you aren't asking for a straight vertical profile, or even for the neck to rise. The horse's nose remains in front of the vertical.

The key point is for the flexion to come from the poll and not from the rising of the upper part of the neck, which would tell you the horse is tucking his nose too severely (possibly behind the bit) and your legs were not quick enough to keep him on the bit.

The moment your horse does flex at the poll, relax your fingers to ease the pressure, but not enough to allow him to begin flattening out. Undoubtedly, he will do this a time or two, so immediately (remembering to use your legs) close your fingers again and, after a response, give slightly.

All this requires a certain tact, for you are teaching

your horse, in this mild way, to hold himself collected by sharing the responsibility. You don't want to hold him by a firm, fixed hand, so you must give slightly (his reward) when he maintains his collection.

These steps lead to that proverbial *lightness* one strives for in training horses, the same lightness which carries over into other specialized training fields with a well-trained horse.

Condition the horse to flexion in short practice sessions. Teach him to utilize it in the other gaits for short periods. When calmness is attained and you *feel* the horse responding automatically, have him flex for more sustained periods of work.

Flexion, to re-emphasize a point, should be a result emanating more from your legs than your hands. The surge of the horse's motion must always be forward. *En avant!* as the French would say, or as other instructors have written—*legs, legs, legs!*

However it is expressed, legs should regulate the forward motion. You neither want to overdrive the horse (certainly not in the mild collection we are speaking of) nor underdrive him. The legs must maintain the necessary balance. And what has been stressed throughout this book, and becomes more important as you progress, is the need to *feel* when the horse is correct.

THE REIN-BACK

For no particular reason, the rein-back has been left for last, although teaching the horse to back too early in his training can cause disturbance of his neck. Besides, like the canter, the rein-back can have a few glaring faults, readily displayed if demanded before the horse has found his balance and is confirmed on the bit.

Poorly executed rein-backs are openly evident (if you care to look) at any horse show. Some horses do not walk backward with deliberate, light steps. They rush back with hind legs sprawled, back sunken and nose either tossed in the air or tucked against the chest. Naturally, they back crookedly. Any of these conditions are seeds for dangerous habits such as rearing, whirling and balking.

There are different ways to teach a horse to rein-back. But there is only one criterion for judging the method: The horse must step back straight, and willingly. Further, if these attributes are present, the horse's leg sequence carries him backward on diagonal pairs, as in the trot.

You may begin teaching the rein-back either mounted or dismounted, but alongside a fence or wall to assist the horse in backing straight. If you choose to teach from the ground, stand to the side of the animal, close to his head, holding a rein in each hand about six inches behind the bit. Gently lower his head and push the reins backward in an easy motion. Touching his leg at the pastern with the toe of your boot helps the horse get the idea.

Don't lean into his mouth, attempting to force his weight to the rear. Use a push, releasing pressure when the horse takes a backward step. Then push on the reins for another step and again release when a step has been taken. You could simultaneously command, *"Back."*

Backing is not a common movement for the horse, so you should keep the lessons short. A few steps a day is sufficient to get the idea to him without having him begin resisting you. After about six lessons, execute the rein-back from the saddle.

If you decide to execute the rein-back initially from the saddle, again place your horse alongside a wall or railing guide. With your horse at the alert halt and your hands lower than usual, holding the reins absolutely even, squeeze your calves easily to stimulate motion from the horse. But before he starts to move forward, begin applying pressure to the rear with your reins until you obtain one step backward. Then release the aids. Again, gather your horse and give your aids, obtaining another step, perhaps two, if he is reining-back smoothly.

After each step, just slightly relax the aids. Then re-apply them for another step, taking and giving when the horse gives, *step by step,* rather than demanding five or six steps in one continuous motion.

When the horse steps back willingly, increase the rein-back to four, five, six and seven steps without stopping between steps. But still relax your aids just slightly for an instant between steps. Speed is not necessary while backing. Slow, deliberate steps, with the legs lifting and clearing the ground (and not sliding through the dirt), is what you should aim for.

The rein-back is a dandy test of the coordination of your aids and *how well* your horse is responding to them. For example (and you should do this after each rein-back), when you have backed the horse to the number of steps you wish, and he is finishing his last step, urge him with more leg aid and reverse the flow of motion forward. In addition to helping harmonize your aids, this also helps the horse keep himself balanced in anticipation of having to move forward. This also makes for a more balanced rein-back.

But you mustn't stop more than twice with the same number of steps backward. In doing so, you could create a habit pattern. The horse doesn't care for this exercise and, understandably enough with horses, if you back five steps about three times in a row, soon he will automatically begin stopping himself on the fifth step. Vary the number of steps backward.

Work for calmness with deliberate cadence. Only an easy opening and closing of the fingers on the reins should be required to keep the horse backing until your legs urge him forward.

Drifting obliquely in the rein-back occurs as a matter of degree. If the horse's stiffness is pronounced and he backs with a definite drift to the right or left, you can use a one-rein correcting aid on the same side of the drift and toward the opposite hip to correct the deviation. For example, say the horse backs toward the left. While the right rein keeps its support to prevent his head from turning, use the left rein (with sufficient pressure) in a line that crosses in front of the withers and toward the right hip. This corrects the deviation without disturbing the front end. When you feel the horse straighten, regain an even contact with the reins and require another backward step—straight—before urging him forward.

An educated horse is one that does well the things he knows, rather than a horse that merely does a lot of things.

If that description fits your animal, he has learned the basic requirements of a fine pleasure horse. And you both have come far.

Even with mistakes granted, only a solid, in-depth attempt at training can teach you the skills necessary to train your next horse even better. While the necessary experience is not easily come by, it is the only way.

Wilhelm Müseler, in an exceptional riding book entitled *Riding Logic*, sums this idea up admirably: "Anybody can learn to ride [he also meant *train*, too, for his book is of that ilk], for riding is nothing but skill. Skill can only be acquired by continual 'trying out' and practice, *but not by imitation of a model.* Once skill has been acquired, however, it should be exercised in 'good form.'"

*My emphasis.—A.A.

CHAPTER
9

EQUESTRIAN TACT

With horses, nothing always works exactly as predicted. If it did, dogmatic formulas for training would be sufficient, without those *buts, ifs, howevers, don'ts* and other qualifiers which attach to the lessons that have gone before. But such is the variety among horses, and the even greater differences of individual training abilities, that a book can only serve as a guide.

The purpose of this book is to assist a novice in gaining confidence in the sometimes tricky application of horse-training principles. Much has been left unsaid (taking a horse into the double bridle, the subtle use of diagonal aids at the canter, or the peculiarities of the horse traveling crookedly at the canter). And while there is *more*, little is accomplished unless an individual's equestrian tact matches the requirements for further work. If it does, then more instruction is hardly required for taking a horse further into training. If it does not, then a hundred books won't help at any level of training.

Hopefully, you will now have been made aware of equestrian tact through the emphasis on learning to *feel*, to adjust and coordinate your aids and to always challenge yourself to draw out more quality from your horse's performance by improving the quality of your aids.

This is the *more* that truly counts; a development of equestrian tact that is never easy to define, but visible whenever you see a superbly performing horse.

Equestrian tact can even offset flaws in one's riding form and allow him to display well-trained horses. For instance, James Fillis, sometimes described as a "monkey on horseback" for his lack of "equitational form," elicited some spectacular feats from his virtuosity and yet abided by all the principles of correct training.

Jumping classes at horse shows often display riders who hardly follow proper riding form and yet soar their horses over enormous jumps.

Why? What is that intangible quality some riders possess that offsets poor form, while others' equally poor form only hinders their horses?

Of course, good form is ideal. It is even indispensable in classic horsemanship. But the question is—why is it that some riders, regardless of any form, are always with their horses and not against them? How do they achieve that very special harmony?

Harmony is an applicable word here, necessary to arrive at a definition of equestrian tact. Defined precisely, it means an agreement of parts or elements, or accord, as of feeling. That's much closer to what we are looking for in a definition of *equestrian tact*. And it's the idea I have literally preached throughout this book in emphasizing the necessity of learning to *feel*.

And while much has been left unsaid, to try and tell everything is impossible. A book can teach you the principles, but it can never develop the qualities that should grow from the principles through proper application and practice.

With students, I have discovered that to try and explain all the contingencies which might occur during some phase of training almost blots out what the response is supposed to look or feel like. Yet the better students quickly sensed for themselves an incorrect response and just as quickly corrected it.

What was it these particular students knew, instinctively, without lecturing, which caused them to display an equestrian tact? The answer: They had discovered the basic ingredient—refinement of the aids.

Now don't remark, "Is that all?" simply because refinement of the aids, like the terms lightness, suppleness and harmony are common expressions. Granted, they are words inscribed on countless pages in equitational literature, almost to the point of numbing their impact. But equestrian tact, in simple language, is the thin line of knowing when an aid, or combination of aids, is enough, not enough or too much.

I am reminded of a passage in an old horse book where the author, discussing grip and balance, says: " . . . grip preserves the balance, which in turn prevents the grip becoming irksome." What a graphic illustration of what I am striving to impress about refined aids.

Refined aids are not necessarily always gentle; they can become rough for disciplinary action. Aids must cause discomfort when required, but how does one distinguish between discomfort and pain unless he or she already knows when an aid is refined rather than weak? Only experience can teach you. And it follows that the collective aids—weight, legs, hands and auxiliary aids such as crop or spur—begin exercising more control in combination than by the intense use of one or two.

With aid refinement, you know when your horse takes the aid sensitively or insensitively. Your refined aids allow you to quickly feel when the aid is adequately sensitive to get a response and not overly sensitive to get none. For example: I referred to developing *lightness,* as does any instruction regarding horses. Lightness is virtually a hymn of equitational achievement. But, *how light* is light? If you're not wary, you may develop lightness to such a refinement (say in the mouth) that the horse actually doesn't know what bit pressure is. Consequently, you might put him in a double bridle and he would practically turn into a star-gazer, flinching at the barest touch of the bit. That's *too* light.

If this sounds contradictory, it is because equitation is, in numerous ways, paradoxical in the use of the aids— at least to the horse. Until you refine the aids, the horse is subjected to an urging-checking situation. With refined aids, urging-checking rarely is applied with the same intensity.

What else does refining the aids accomplish? That it improves your ability as a rider and trainer is obvious, but stemming from that ability are many other benefits. Possibly most important is the recognition of stiffness caused by conformation faults as opposed to stiffness which signals resistance. The horse may be obeying the reins, but could still have a numb mouth, which could signify resistance from the quarters, back or shoulder, and should be recognized and attended to promptly.

Refining the ride permits you to *feel* that a stiff horse cannot bend as easily or readily as one that is supple. Such a horse cannot, for example, be expected to ride into the arena corners as deeply without such evasive responses as the inside shoulder "falling in," or a rider not over-reacting, causing the haunches to fall out toward the arc of the corner.

Refinement of the ride allows you to "put a horse together," with all parts working smoothly "calm, forward, straight."

Also, it makes you more expert at sizing-up horses and deciding how to approach the training of each. A rider's equestrian tact is ever flexible, making him realize one cannot deal with every horse as if it were the ideal illustrated in most training manuals. Some horses will be sensitive to aids. Others, most often mares, tighten their muscles in disobedience to those same aids. You'll learn that a horse whose head sets off its neck at a 45-degree angle will respond in gaits and flexions differently from one whose set is flat out.

And there is this pleasant benefit which was mentioned in an earlier chapter: Your particular equestrian tact opens the way to better appraisal of opinions expressed in various horse books. You may, even now, understand why one book advocates teaching flexions and collection after a horse has learned to "go forward" with a natural head and neck carriage, and another suggests putting the horse in a double bridle after only a preliminary work in the snaffle.

Both methods work. But the one you choose depends upon the method which best suits your level of equestrian tact, because equestrian tact filters through and reflects at all levels of riding and training horses. It is the polish, the quality, the *how well* which only you can develop. It is, in a word—*horsemanship*.

And the pleasure of it all, from the moment you first step into a saddle to learn to ride, or to train your first horse, your sense of *feel,* your equestrian tact, your horse-manship, can only grow better and better. The challenge for improvement always shines a reach ahead of you as you go on and on.

That is the joy of horses and horsemanship. All you need is confidence—and a love for horses.

THE PLEASURES OF HORSE BOOKS

Reflecting on this brief introduction for learning to understand and train horses, I feel I might have suggested a harsh attitude about the usefulness of books than I truly intended.

I didn't mean to negate books, training books especially, but to emphasize that without having first obtained some experiences which establishes your particular *feel* with horses, much of what can be instructive through books can be confusing and lost. And although the expression, "you can't learn from books," is repeated often enough, I insist one can derive many benefits if it is coupled with an intense desire to learn.

After all, one does not inherit an ability with horses, contrary to the adage, "a born horseman." True, some are quicker to grasp the fundamental *feel*, but I have never witnessed a slow learner who did not achieve proficiency if the desire to learn was intense enough. This desire in itself often leads to book reading, and a learning which does not necessarily need to rely on purely instructional books.

When I look back and reflect on the horse books I have read, reread, and was mesmerized by, I am rather glad that I lived my youthful horse experiences somewhat vicariously through books. I would have missed some high horse adventures otherwise.

While I recall that period as a melancholy one—not a unique experience for avid horse fans who are literally horseless in a metropolitan city—to have had horses then would likely have offset any need to seek them through books in the public library. Since the few peddlers' horses then still in the city were not the sleek, beautiful horses of the mind's eye, I turned to books.

The first book I actually recall reading was C. S. Anderson's *Black, Bay and Chestnut,* brief true stories of famous horses on the track and in the steeplechase. I think what delighted me most in Anderson's book, besides his artistic renderings of the horses, is the manner in which he wrote his profiles of twenty favorite horses. Each horse was described with the idea of presenting an individual accomplishment, personality, quirk or character that made the horse famous. Thus, War Admiral, a Triple Crown winner; Ugly, a United States Army show jumper; Troublemaker, a steeplechaser who died attempting one of the awesome jumps of that sport, all come alive in personality and feats that made the book memorable to a young, horse-crazy mind.

But with Carl Raswan I literally went on a magic carpet and shared exotic adventures in the Arabian Desert with Bedouins and their Arab horses. *Black Tents of Arabia* was the first excursion. The search for the perfect Arab horse, who became Ghazal, in *Drinkers of the Wind,* was even more inspiring. I read these magical books at a time when Arab horses were so scarce in the United States that they were more myth than reality. Raswan wrote with so much sincere inspiration about the Arab horses that, even today, the Arab is for me a standard of excellence.

The librarian at Yonkers, New York, became aware of my passion for reading about horses. I had virtually read all that the library had on its shelves. I remember asking her if any new horse books would be forthcoming. She answered uncertainly, but did add that many books were stored in the basement because there was a shortage of stack space. She would see what was down there.

I'm glad she did; otherwise I would have missed Colonel Theodore Dodge's *Riders of Many Lands,* a very old book even then. Though I realized that the times had changed since Dodge wrote his book, it was still fun and exciting. We toured North Africa with the French and Spahi Cavalry and their Barb and Arab horses, and continued around the world to visit other horsemen and learn of their horses, customs, horse sports and lore.

Another world of horses was opened to me when I came upon *The Horses of the Conquest,* by R. B. Cunningham-Graham. Here I accompanied the first horses to come ashore on the North American continent with their

Spanish explorers. The story is a mixture of triumph, because of the horses, and of sadness, as the horses died one by one in the battles that led to the conquest of Mexico. More precious than gold were these horses, and no wonder the conquistadors took such personal concern for their small *caballado*. Under Graham's skillful pen the horses are a living entity, and the volume qualifies as literature in a mass of similar horse books that do not quite deserve that distinction.

Graham was provocative (some say even eccentric). He led me to other works of his which favored the Gaucho and his horses of the Pampas; and to Tschiffely and Mancha and Gato, in their ride from Argentina to the eastern United States, in *Tschiffely's Ride*. An epic adventure.

I could go on, but it is the pleasures of horse books I want to mention, not what I have read. But let me mention one more book, James Reynolds' *A World of Horses*. Odd, now that I think about my first reaction to Reynolds, that I didn't care for it and found it difficult to read. Later, however, when I looked through it again, reading a section or chapter, I felt myself warming to it. It was like not caring for someone you meet the first time, but becoming more sociable after you get to know the person better. Reynolds was an artist and follower of Thoroughbred sports and his book is a very personal talk about one man's love for horses. You truly have to let yourself go with him. Once you do, Reynolds is fascinating. Here is a random selection:

"When my friends in Virginia, Canada, or Ireland gather around an open fire, food and drink at hand, no lights up, just the leaping light and shadow of ragged red and orange flames licking the big logs in the fireplace, the talk may very likely turn to steeplechasing. For one thing, all who know me know it is the subject closest to my heart. It is where I live. . . . The look of the steeplechaser is very definite. . . ."

And with that, Reynolds takes you to his world of one

of the toughest of horse competitions, where the Thoroughbred is supreme. As I have said, Reynolds is very personal and once you accept him for his ways, it is a delight to be with him.

If I were to try and offer some succinct appraisal of the value of horse books I would probably fail. Anything as varied as the roles a horse can be put to, and the enormous amount of history behind him, is bound to give rise to numerous slants of appreciation. But possibly it is just this factor itself that lends to the pleasure of horse books—to participate in other horse activities than one's own and to see how others look at horses and the particular joy they derive from their sport.

For example, we all can't be active in Thoroughbred racing, but we cheat ourselves of one of the most consistently exciting horse activities that take place on breeding farms and on the tracks if we ignore what is being written in this field.

Think about those generations of horsemen who have developed and trained the Thoroughbred horse. Think of the theories that have evolved in breeding for speed, and the great progenitors of the breed, and the enormous amount of comment that has been made by turf writers, and historians. They compare and analyze the great ones; they continually wonder at the speed demons on the track who were not so good at stud, as Native Dancer.

Consider Man o' War: Will there ever be unanimous opinion as to his greatness? I hope not. The controversy in words written about him is far more fascinating, and lead you to live and relive his exploits from many points of view. B. K. Beckwith in his book, *Step and Go Together*, wrote about Man o' War through an interview with his trainer, Lou Fuestel. He told Beckwith about the time Man o' War won the Lawrence Realization at Belmont in what Beckwith prefaced as the "most outstanding display of arrogant annihilation I ever witnessed on the track."

Man o' War had been pitted against a contender

named Hoodwink. This is how Beckwith remembered the race when the chestnut wonder turned for home on the long stretch at Belmont track.

" . . . he was one of the most magnificent and appalling sights you ever saw. He was like a big red sheet of flame running before a prairie wind, and every bound he took opened up more daylight. When he hit the wire, hard held, Hoodwink was almost an eighth of a mile behind him. The time for the mile and five-eights was 2:40⅘, a world's record which stood for twenty-seven years."

Reading about Man o' War today is like listening to a fantasy about the sort of race horse track men dream about—a once in a lifetime fabulous runner. He was far ahead of his time, and interestingly enough, for all the track records Big Red scored no one knows how fast he really could have run. Fuestel told Beckwith that the horse was never let out all the way, and still, if Man o' War had started his fourth season, he would have been handicapped with 140 pounds. Thus, he was retired as a three-year-old. Can you imagine the speculation that has occurred about what would have happened if he had started again the following season, stronger and more developed?

As fabulous as his racing career, his stud career is almost equal. He created a fabulous dynasty—Battleship, War Admiral, Blockade (he won the Maryland Hunt Cup three times) and hundreds of others sons and daughters. Think of this, too, in this age of leg problems that plague the Thoroughbred—Man o' War, according to Fuestel, never had so much as a pimple on his legs! But, remembers Fuestel, Man o' War was temperamental—"would peel the shirt off you if you weren't looking . . ."

Performance and personality; that's the stuff that brings horses to vivid life. Man o' War, Seabiscuit, Citation, Swaps, the fiery Nashua, who would never make his move until he felt like it (and jockey Eddie Arcaro often wanted to punch the horse), make for exciting reading in books and reminiscences about the turf world.

Arcaro wrote one, *I Ride to Win,* and the point of view is that of the jockey. You learn that a jockey just doesn't sit on the horse and guide him. A lot of strategy and watching the pace goes into riding a race horse. Arcaro rode Whirlaway, a top horse who had the bad habit of bearing out to the outside rail. Arcaro was taken aback when just before a race Whirlaway's trainer placed a one-eyed blinker on the horse. Would it work? Arcaro wrote: "He literally took off, nearly catapulting me out of the saddle. As he stretched his legs, I felt as if I were flying through the air."

More jockeys should write of their experiences in the saddle. Shoemaker, Longden, Hartack would have a lot to say about the horses they have blazed to glory upon in the past decades, and the glory they just missed because of a bad riding judgment, a setback or reverse. These too make for the drama of the sport, and a lot of heartbreak.

The best thing about books on horses is that there is no end to where they can take you. The adventure is world wide. Books on the Grand National, books about cavalry, books about fox hunting, if they are well written, can take you along in the authors' adventures and exploits. I've never followed the hounds in a fox hunt, under a sturdy 16.2 Thoroughbred, galloping across country and jumping over brush and fence as the pack gives full cry. But I have lived it through books about fox hunting, just as if I were feeling the long strides of a gallop myself, and have learned that fox hunting is a world unto itself with particular idiom, custom and dress.

For sheer excitement, second by second, the world of show jumping has its own special distinction. Pat Smythe, England's high scoring rider, conveys the thrills of international competition in her *Jumping Around the World.*

For youthful spontaneity and a marvelous horse adventure, *Canadian Entry* has much appeal, particularly for teen-age girls. This book is about Christilot Hanson, a Canadian who learned dressage of Olympic caliber under tough German masters and then went on to an impressive showing at the Tokyo Olympics. The story of Christilot and her horse, Bonheur, is good reading for young people interested in skilled horsemanship.

I liked even more *The Will to Win*. If you haven't heard of Tommy Smith and Thoroughbred Jay Trump you have missed the saga of a hard-won triumph. Smith and Jay Trump became the first American pair to win the gruelling Grand National at Aintree, England, in 1965. Author Jane McIlvaine gives her readers one of the best insights into the not-too-well-known world of steeplechasing. The story is a very human one of how Tom dedicated himself to his dream of winning the Grand National, and did.

And if rodeo is your slant, one can become part of the legacy of this tough sport with Gene Lamb's *Man, Beast and Dust*, or with Foghorn Clancy's *My Fifty Years in Rodeo*. As in racing, rodeo buffs argue who were the best riders, or if Steamboat was better than Midnight, or if Five Minutes to Midnight was better than either of the two. Willard Porter's *13 Flat* is an insight into the roping sport that has its special requirements and allows one to see the horse from another view. And if you're a fan of the Standardbred, books such as *Dan Patch, Big G* or *Bret Hanover* are familiar pace-setting names in the development of the Standardbred and racing speed. Like Thoroughbreds, Standardbreds are exciting precision speed tools.

Perspective. Maybe this is what horse books can offer their enlightened readers through an exposure to other ideas about horses. This leads me to another class of books, books which instruct.

Edward Spinola, in his introduction to *Breeding the Race Horse*, by F. Tesio, wrote: ". . . experience is not easily come by and many years and much hard work can be wasted by starting from scratch instead of the foundations which others have painstakingly established."

Thus the established works are the best to consult, although, as I have indicated, these can sometimes be confusing until you have found your own way with horses. Nonetheless, certain authors' works deserve room in the library of any horseman who is deserving of the name *horseman*.

Captain Vladimer Littauer, a Russian emigré with cavalry background, has distilled over forty years of training, teaching, comparing and synthesizing classic and forward schools of riding. His major aim is the jumper and cross-country horse, and his *Commonsense Horsemanship* is a major contribution to this equitational form.

One can dwell for years over how Littauer has measured the horse and prescribed its training. In his later, and more brief, *Schooling Your Horse,* he presents just enough information to assist the part-time rider in developing his horse without losing the fundamental strains that weave his philosophy in his major work. Both will influence equitational opinion for years to come.

Akin to Captain Littauer's inquiring spirit is that of the late General Harry D. Chamberlin, also of cavalry conditioning (U.S.).

After extended study abroad at the military equitation schools in Italy and France, he returned to the United States and revitalized the doctrines at Fort Riley, Kansas. He wrote two books: *Riding and Schooling Horses* (some concepts have been superceded), and his more enduring work, *Training Hunters, Jumpers and Hacks.* Together they are probably the finest an American has offered to the bibliography of equitational literature.

Like Littauer, Chamberlin aims his study to the jumper and field horse. He never denies the heritage of the classic schools, but used what he felt was beneficial to create willing and bold jumpers and cross-country mounts. So substantial is his approach to training that many concepts are acceptable to the training of the western horse. What Chamberlin has to say about the debilitating loss of calmness and jumpers rushing their fences is equally applicable to Western stock horses that rush a show pattern or cattle.

His remarks about good hands and educated hands, while not new, actually (Chamberlin himself suggests "nothing in equitation is new"), certainly takes on a fresh, clearly presented appraisal.

He has influenced more-recent American writers, as Louis Taylor in his *Ride American,* a sensible overall look at riding, and John Richard Young's, *The Schooling of the Western Horse.* Each, however, adds dozens of kernals of information to suit the needs of particular audiences and the part-time pleasure horse rider of today.

In the field of classic equitation many books bid for attention. For the most part, I will give my eyes to the urban writings of the late Alois Podhajsky, former director of the Spanish Riding School.

No one can dispute his enthusiasm for the horse, its training, or its ability—except himself. His writings, from line to line, from volume to volume, ring with a love of horses that is absent from many clinical approaches.

Podhajsky's *The Complete Training of Horse and Rider,* is a tome certain to become a standard work on classic equitation. And without belittling it one iota, I give a slight preference (because of my particular interests) to his lighter and more delightful, *My Horses, My Teachers.*

Years ago I read the horse memoirs of Will James, the cowboy artist and writer. In his, *Horses I have Known,* James told about broncs and cow ponies that educated him in his particular world of horses. *My Horses, My Teachers,* is a similar excursion, although at another end of the vast spectrum of horses and the ways men use them.

Podhajsky tells of his first acquaintance with horses, as a son of an Army officer, at cavalry barracks. Later, as an officer himself in the Austro-Hungarian cavalry, he recounts the horses that shared his career. How his horses educated him, and how he learned to understand horses and their training from the horse's point of view, makes *My Horses, My Teachers* a most instructive book and completely enjoyable to read.

I like this particular observation about one named Winky:

"When Winky made correct transitions from one pace to the other by increasing, as from the trot into the canter, and by reducing, as from the trot into the walk, he began to reveal a very brilliant extended trot. Of course I was pleased with it and made the mistake every rider easily commits and demanded too many and too long periods at the extended trot. But suddenly I felt Winky stiffen against the pushing aids of my legs, which was a sign of alarm to me. I contented myself with a few good steps and brought work to an end. Forty Wink's owner was of the opinion that I had given in to his naughtiness but she was mistaken. The fault was mine; I had demanded too much. The young horse had no other choice. He could not tell me: 'Stop! I am at the end of my strength!'

"Whenever difficulties appear, the first thing the rider must do is to ask himself: does the horse not want to execute my demands, does he not understand what I want, or is he physically unable to carry them out? The rider's conscience must find the answer. If there is any doubt it is much better to assume that the horse is unable to carry out the commands and leave it at that, which is much wiser than obtaining the exercise by force. An omission is never of such bad consequence as an injustice."

Podhajsky has said more in that brief passage than dozens of other books have suggested.

Points of view and perspective: that is the quality of significant books. In looking over my own library and glancing at a volume here and there, I see other varied titles that provide perspective, thought, and pleasure in their reading: Margaret Cabell Self's, *Horsemastership;* and Gordon Wright's, *Learning to Ride, Hunt and Show. Fundamentals of Riding* by Gregor de Romaszkan and *Modern*

Riding by S. R. Kulesza are exceptionally interesting as both authors are former members of the Polish cavalry—another equitational point of view.

For an historic analysis of the great writers, from Xenophon to the present day, W. Sidney Felton's, *Masters of Equitation* is a succinct presentation, while E. Hartley Edward's book, *Saddlery,* is necessary to understand the vast array of horse equipment, bits, bridles, and bitting arrangements and the basic part these play in equitation.

All assist to provide the wherefores and reflections for the inquiring horseman. Like actual practice, which the dedicated horseman is forever challenged to, books offer the encouragement to reflect and compare, and to improve one's horsemanship.

INDEX

A

B

D

S

X

Y

DE